To Susie Carter,

Continue to Be Financially Fit!

Agape Love

Rev. Dr. Donna Taylor

Centinnes to be

Friendly !!!

Hope so

Rev. Dr. Horace Taylor

Financial Empowerment in the African American Church

Examining the Attitudes of Congregants to Adopt Christian Stewardship and Debt Management Principles

Rev. Dr. Donna Taylor

BALBOA
PRESS
A DIVISION OF HAY HOUSE

Copyright © 2018 Rev. Dr. Donna Taylor.

All rights reserved. No part of this book may be used or reproduced by any means, graphic, electronic, or mechanical, including photocopying, recording, taping or by any information storage retrieval system without the written permission of the author except in the case of brief quotations embodied in critical articles and reviews.

This book is a work of non-fiction. Unless otherwise noted, the author and the publisher make no explicit guarantees as to the accuracy of the information contained in this book and in some cases, names of people and places have been altered to protect their privacy.

Balboa Press books may be ordered through booksellers or by contacting:

Balboa Press
A Division of Hay House
1663 Liberty Drive
Bloomington, IN 47403
www.balboapress.com
1 (877) 407-4847

Because of the dynamic nature of the Internet, any web addresses or links contained in this book may have changed since publication and may no longer be valid. The views expressed in this work are solely those of the author and do not necessarily reflect the views of the publisher, and the publisher hereby disclaims any responsibility for them.

The author of this book does not dispense medical advice or prescribe the use of any technique as a form of treatment for physical, emotional, or medical problems without the advice of a physician, either directly or indirectly. The intent of the author is only to offer information of a general nature to help you in your quest for emotional and spiritual well-being. In the event you use any of the information in this book for yourself, which is your constitutional right, the author and the publisher assume no responsibility for your actions.

Any people depicted in stock imagery provided by Thinkstock are models, and such images are being used for illustrative purposes only.
Certain stock imagery © Thinkstock.

Print information available on the last page.

ISBN: 978-1-5043-9386-7 (sc)
ISBN: 978-1-5043-9388-1 (hc)
ISBN: 978-1-5043-9387-4 (e)

Library of Congress Control Number: 2018900184

Balboa Press rev. date: 01/16/2018

CONTENTS

ABSTRACT vii
ACKNOWLEDGEMENTS ix
PREFACE xi
DEDICATION xiii
GLOSSARY xv
EPIGRAPH xix
FOREWARD xxi
INTRODUCTION xxiii

CHAPTER
    1. MINISTRY FOCUS 1
    2. THE STATE OF THE ART IN THIS MINISTRY MODEL 22
    3. THEOLOGICAL FOUNDATION 34
    4. METHODOLOGY 37
    5. FIELD EXPERIENCE 45
    6. SUMMARY, CONCLUSIONS, AND REFLECTIONS 54
    7. EPILOGUE 61

APPENDIX
    A. FINANCIAL LITERACY QUESTIONS 63
    B. FINANCIAL WHEEL 65
    C. FINANCIAL LITERACY EDUCATION PROGRAM SECTORS 67
    D. MASLOW'S HIERARCHY OF NEEDS 69
    E. MASLOW'S LAW EXPLANATION 71
    F. FLOWS OF SOCIAL INFLUENCE ON CONSUMER FINANCIAL BEHAVIOR 75

G.	STEWARDSHIP AND DEBT MANAGEMENT - PRE/POST SURVEY	77
H.	WILCOXON SIGNED RANK TEST RESULTS	81
I.	FINANCIAL LITERACY TRAINING	83
J.	FINANCIAL EMPOWERMENT – MARKETING STRATEGY	91
K.	CHURCH BULLETIN INSERT - EARLY PHASE	93
L.	CHURCH BULLETIN INSERT – LATE PHASE	95
M.	POST CARD INVITATION	97
N.	EMAIL AND TEXT MESSAGES	99
O.	WORKSHOP #1 GOD'S BLUEPRINT FOR PERSONAL FINANCE	101
P.	WORKSHOP #2 GODLY TOOLS FOR DEBT PREVENTION	107
Q.	WORKSHOP #3 GODLY TOOLS FOR DEBT MANAGEMENT	111
R.	WORKSHOP #4 A GODLY PLAN: SAVING FOR EMERGENCIES	117
S.	WORKSHOP #5 ESTATE PLANNING: FAMILY DIALOGUE & LEGACY	123
T.	WORKSHOP#6 APPLYING STEWARDSHIP AND DEBT MANAGEMENT PRINCIPLES	129
U.	PARTICIPANTS' COMMENTS AT THE CONCLUSION OF THE FINANCIAL EMPOWERMENT WORKSHOP	135

BIBLIOGRAPHY ... 137

ABSTRACT

EXAMINING THE KNOWLEDGE OF
CONGREGANTS TO ADOPT
STEWARDSHIP AND DEBT MANAGEMENT PRINCIPLES
TO FORMULATE A FINANCIAL
EMPOWERMENT
MINISTRY
By
Donna Wells-Taylor, D. Min.
Virginia University of Lynchburg, 2014

Core Faculty Advisor
Dr. Carlton Jackson

The purpose of this quantitative research was to examine congregants' knowledge of stewardship and debt management principles. Ten congregants participated in a six-week intervention and data was collected using a 20-question survey with a 5-point Likert scale. Hypothesis: If selected members of the FABCF congregation are exposed to stewardship principles by direct instruction, then there will be an increase in knowledge among membership to establish a Financial Empowerment Ministry. Data was analyzed using the Wilcoxon signed-rank test in SPSS with $p\ value$ <0.05. Congregants' knowledge improved after stewardship and debt management training, and a Financial Empowerment Ministry was launched.

ACKNOWLEDGEMENTS

The author wishes to extend sincere thanks to Rev. Dr. Daniel Lloyd Brown, the Pastor and Founder of First Agape Baptist Community of Faith for his support, guidance, and spiritual leadership during this project and to me throughout the years. I am grateful to my husband, and my friend, David Leon Taylor, my contextual associate who has provided a unique insight to stewardship and kingdom building. Dr. Carlton Jackson, my core advisor instilled in me the importance of academic excellence. Dr. James Coleman, my Core II Reader, instilled the importance of being an equipped practitioner of the church. Dr. Marshall Mays, the Dean of the School of Religion, expanded my knowledge of the best practices for an effective preaching ministry. Dr. Clarence Cross, your historic perspective on Civil Rights and economic empowerment for African Americans is particularly relevant to the Black Church during this time of economic uncertainty. To Deacon Hebert McKoy, my contextual associate and Deacon Chair, your enthusiasm, knowledge, and dedication are quite exceptional. Rev. LeRoy Hill, my peer, you possess a Pastors' heart and a compassion for God's people and their struggles. You have a unique perspective on the impact of Black Wall Street during the most tumultuous era in the history of our nation. Dr. Gregory Fant, my colleague and an expert statistician, your counsel has been invaluable. Dr. Lorenzo McFarland, my colleague, you have shared your experiences, which have been profound and noteworthy. Rev. Louie Jenkins, always an encourager and have always been supportive to my family and me. Lillie Bethea, my maternal grandmother who prayed for me. Her wisdom, faith, and love were a pillar of strength and taught me to strive despite the obstacles. Sharon Thorne, my friend, you have the gift of exhortation, which is invaluable in the Kingdom of God and to my ministry. To Dr. Elva Ward your commitment to the doctoral learners is truly a gift from God. To my parents Vivian and Sylvester McCray who instilled in me to never give up, the importance of developing inner strength, and to be resourceful and independent. To Rev. Dr. Nathaniel Tyler Lloyd, the deceased Pastor of Trinity Baptist Church in the Bronx, New York, who served in the same pulpit for over forty years; a true man of God, who impacted my early spiritual development and the community-at-large, where more than ten thousand souls called you, Pastor. May you forever rest in peace.

PREFACE

Since African Americans arrived in North America, there has been an impetus to survive in spite of limited financial and material resources. The signing of the Emancipation Proclamation in 1863 was a pivotal moment for freed men and women who recognized the importance of pooling their resources to build great churches and universities. In 2014, African Americans possessed spending power of more than one trillion dollars, which equaled the economy of Canada and the United States foreign investments. Despite this economic milestone, the mortgage crisis of 2008 - 2009 reduced the wealth of African Americans by fifty percent. Clearly, it is incumbent upon African Americans to begin to redirect their financial resources to increase their personal savings and investments to plan for financial shocks that are inevitable. The church can be a catalyst to empower African Americans to manage debt, to save for emergencies, and to establish a financial legacy for future generations.

DEDICATION

I dedicate my research to my husband David Leon Taylor, the inspiration for my writing and our life together. David, because you are a loving and devoted supporter as well as a detailed and careful editor, I am able to complete this work. Your love and encouragement is the catalyst that turned my dreams into a reality. As a faithful companion in the ministry, your wisdom and insight has helped me to find the strength to keep striving. Thank you from the bottom of my heart for being there for me.

GLOSSARY

Bankruptcy - A situation where an individual is incapable of settling his/her debts and has petitioned a court to reduce or eliminate the debt.

Bequest - The act of giving assets such as cash, property, or stocks to a beneficiary through a will.

Certificate of Deposit – CD - A certificate issued as a receipt for funds deposited at a bank or other financial institution for a specific term, which also stands as a promise to repay interest on the funds and to repay the capital amount.

Credit Union - A mutual association or non-profit financial institution formed by people with a common affiliation such as employees, a trade union or religious group in which pooled saving are made. The funds are invested for appreciation and members may borrow at competitive prices.

First Agape Baptist Community of Faith (FABCF) is the context referenced throughout the document and will be referred to as FABCF in the document.

Debt - Money owed by an individual or company to another individual or company. All forms of debt imply intent to repay an amount owed by a specific date.

Endowment - A gift such as money or property to an institution, such as a museum, university or hospital, for a given purpose.

Financial Advisor - A professional person qualified to give advice to clients regarding investments such as life insurance, pensions, mutual funds/unit trusts and taxation.

Foreclosure - The procedure by which a homeowner forfeits his/her property to a lender (mortgagee) following default.

Gentrification - to convert (a deteriorated or aging area in a city) to a more affluent middle-class neighborhood, by remodeling dwellings, resulting in increased property values and in displacement of the poor.

Gross National Product (GNP) -The value of all goods and services produced by a country.

Individual Retirement Account (IRA) - In the U.S., a tax-deferred retirement savings account which may be set up by people in employment.

401(k) - Is a type of company-sponsored tax-deferred retirement plan. It is a salary reduction plan, in which the employee agrees to contribute a certain percentage of wages to the 401(k) plan instead of receiving it as compensation.

Internet Banking - A service provided by banks enabling customers to conduct banking transactions through their personal computer and telephone. This system allows instant access to bank balances and the provision for transferring funds.

Mortgage - A loan in which the borrower (the mortgagor) offers a property and land as security to the lender (the mortgagee) until the loan is repaid.

Mutual Loan - A collective investment scheme operated by an investment company that enables small private investors to invest in a diversified portfolio of shares, bonds and other securities.

Predatory Lending - An unscrupulous lending practice that targets low-income or otherwise vulnerable people. Predatory lending involves making high-cost loans to borrowers based on their level of assets and not on their ability to repay the debt.

This practice also may require a borrower to refinance the loan repeatedly, which lets the lender charge high points and fees. Another predatory practice is using fraud or deceit to conceal the true cost of the loan from an unsophisticated borrower.

Prosperity Gospel or Theology - A religious belief that wealth is a divine reward for a person's faith in God.

Purchasing Power - Tracking an index of consumer prices and comparing can assess the change in purchasing between two different periods.

Upside Down Mortgage - When someone owes more on their home or property than it is currently worth in the market; also called being "underwater" or having "negative equity." An example of an upside down mortgage is when the market value of a home drops, leaving the owners unable to sell the home for enough money to pay off their mortgage loan.

Will - A document that sets out how a person wishes his/her estate or property to be dispersed after his/her death.

Harriman's Financial Dictionary, Edited by Simon Briscoe and Jane Fuller, Harriman House, 2013. A financial dictionary with over 2, 600 essential financial terms.

The New Oxford American Dictionary, Oxford University Press, Second Edition, 2005. A comprehensive Dictionary of terms.

Webster's New World Finance and Investment Dictionary, Fourth Edition. 2003. By the editors of Webster's New World Dictionary. By Barbara J. Etzel.

EPIGRAPH

Many people are in the dark when it comes to money, and I'm going to turn on the lights.

Suze Orman

FOREWARD

It is a privilege to observe visionary response to a pressing need in our society. We often applaud those who recognize a life-pressing situation and respond by thoughtful solution.

We therefore applaud and encourage the reading of a work that has responded to a pressing problem in our universal church family. Those of us who are pastors, leaders and parishioners realize that in the last five (5) to ten (10) years there has been a financial strain on our churches due to a lack of consistent finance in our church life giving. We recognize that in most churches we have lost income approximately 20 to 40 percent. This has naturally affected Church life programs.

This work addresses this financial church dilemma with thought and solution. Therefore, it is a must read for Pastors, Lay Leaders, Financial Boards, and Church Committees. This work by Rev. Dr. Donna Taylor has the potential for helping our Churches deal with this present financial dilemma. I recommend this work to you and your faith based organization!

Rev. Dr. Daniel L. Brown, PhD.
Pastor, First Agape Baptist Community of Faith
Alexandria, Virginia

INTRODUCTION

On Sunday, October 3, 1999, Rev. Dr. Daniel Lloyd Brown became the pastor and founder of First Agape Baptist Community of Faith in Alexandria, Virginia.[1] On April 2, 2000 the moderator of the Northern Virginia Baptist Association (NVBA), Rev. Dr. Kenny Smith, officially recognized First Agape Baptist Community of Faith as a *church* within the City of Alexandria.[2] First Agape Baptist Community of Faith was established as a tithing church and dedicated for the sole purpose of kingdom building.[3]

Rev. Brown instructed the congregants, "To think about the Will of a perfect, all powerful and loving God who uplifts his people and the empowerment of the Holy Spirit for those who desire to grow spiritually."[4] The church was named, "Agape," which is the unconditional love of Jesus Christ and exemplifies the "Great Commission," that states, "Go ye therefore into all the world and preach the gospel of Jesus Christ (Matthew 28:18-28)."

The intent of this research is to share the interconnectedness between the knowledge of stewardship and debt management principles that can be utilized in every facet of religious life. To date, First Agape Baptist Community of Faith has experienced tremendous financial blessings as a tithing church. Over the last decade, many of the previous generation of tithers have gone home to be with the Lord. Generally speaking, the giving pattern of the younger generation has leveled off. Although the diaconate ministry provides stewardship presentations every Sunday, to inform

---

[1] History of First Agape Baptist Community of Faith in Alexandria, Virginia.
[2] Ibid.
[3] Daniel L. Brown, *Church Planting*, Red Lead Press, 2013
[4] Ibid.

and educate congregants, this effort appears to have limited influence on increasing the overall giving pattern within the church. Most important, congregants confided in the author that their desire to give more was constrained by consumer debt and financial hardships. Since that time, the writer has explored the use of teaching stewardship principles to manage consumer debt among congregants at First Agape Baptist Community of Faith. In discussions with several congregants, it appears financial literacy was the origin of these financial challenges including substantial credit card debt.

A report published by the Organization for Economic Cooperation and Development (OECD 2005) found that, "Financial illiteracy is a widespread problem reaching most countries, certainly those on which there is reliable data."[5] Financial literacy is a concern that is recognized by economists, business leaders, educators, politicians, and clergy who seek unique ways to address this important issue. Every segment of the population is adversely affected by financial illiteracy. "In the United States, those facing the most challenges with financial literacy are the young, elderly, women, African-Americans, Hispanics, the least educated, and those living in rural areas."[6]

Low financial literacy is partly due to the scarcity of formal programs to educate American adult consumers about the growing responsibility of making complex financial decisions. "Whether it is due to the stubbornness of entrenched behaviors, the release of pent-up consumer demand, or other factors, Americans are spending more, saving less, and still carrying credit card debt."[7] The economic recession and the mortgage crisis of 2008-09 raised our awareness regarding the importance of financial literacy.

Chapter one outlines the ministry focus to include the historical background of the context, First Agape Baptist Community of Faith in Alexandria, Virginia with an emphasis on financial literacy as it relates to

---

[5] Robert I. Lerman. and Elizabeth Bell, *Financial Literacy Strategies Where Do We Go From Here?* Opportunity and Ownership Project, The Urban Institute, Report No. 1, 2006.

[6] Ibid..

[7] National Foundation for Credit Counseling (NFCC), *The 2011 Consumer Financial Literacy Final Report*, 2011. Harris Interaction Inc. Public Relations Group accessed online September 20, 2012.

congregants within the local church. This research is designed to expose the pervasive problem of financial illiteracy in the United States and more specifically among congregants in the local church.

Chapter two outlines the state of the art in this ministry model and the literature review that supports the importance of providing financial literacy education programs within a faith-based context. The goal is to promote financial literacy in the church as an impetus to equip congregants to make informed financial decisions. Financial literacy skills also have long-term implications for managing church finances as it pertains to making short and long-term financial goals.

Chapter three outlines the theoretical foundation and the scriptural basis for congregants to learn and apply stewardship and debt management principles in accordance with the scriptures. Stewardship principles are a valuable resource for believers according to the scriptures, which are inspired by God and the power of the Holy Spirit to edify the body of Christ, the church.

Chapter four outlines the quantitative research methodology, utilizing a pre and post survey instrument with a 5-point Likert scale to measure congregants' knowledge of stewardship and debt management principles after participation in financial literacy skills training. Data analysis was conducted using the Wilcoxon signed-ranked test in SPSS, with results that were statistically significant.

Chapter five outlines the writer's field experience with a detailed description of the research to include lesson plans, learning objectives, and the chronology of activities that occurred during each training session. At the conclusion of the six-week intervention, the participants were recognized and honored the following day during Sunday morning worship service. Certificates were presented to each of the participants, facilitators, and Rev. Dr. Daniel L. Brown, as Pastor and adjunct faculty at First Agape Baptist Community of Faith.

Chapter six summarizes the research and its implications, the conclusion, and reflections with recommendations for future researchers.

CHAPTER ONE

Ministry Focus

Reliance on Christian stewardship principles to manage all resources is clearly documented in the scriptures.[8] According to God's word, fiscal responsibility is proclaimed as a virtue. In addition, obedience to God's word is the basis for managing personal finances and making sound financial decisions. Joyner (1993) refers to Luke 6:38 - a key stewardship principle. "Give and it shall be given unto you; good measure, pressed down, shaken together, and running over. For with the same measure that ye mete withal it shall be measured to you again."[9] Utilizing wisdom and spiritual discernment to manage personal finances in accordance with stewardship principles, as outlined in the scriptures, is paramount in the life of the believer.

Applying stewardship principles in the area of financial literacy equips the congregant to manage their personal finances more effectively. Lois Vitt et al., (2001) defined personal financial literacy, "As the ability to read, analyze, manage, and communicate about personal financial conditions that affect [their] material well being and respond competently to life events."[10] The level of financial literacy one may possess can be measured

---

[8] Romans 13:7-8 - NIV all scripture references will be from the NIV unless otherwise notified.

[9] Ronnie D. Joyner, *Breaking Free From Finanical Bondage – A Biblical Plan to Take Control of Your Finance*s (Ronnie Joyner Ministries, Inc. 1993).

[10] Lois Vitt et al., *Personal Finance and the Rush to Competence: Financial Literacy Education in the U.S.* (A National Field Study Commissioned and Supported by The Fannie Mae Foundation, Institue for Socio-Financial Studies, 2001).

based upon successful responses to three basic questions. According to Lusardi and Mitchell (2014), "The ability to evaluate numeracy, understand inflation, and compounding interest are factors that determine financial literacy."[11] Responding correctly to each of these three survey questions demonstrates one's ability to make financial decisions with a basic level of competency. (Appendix A)

Financial literacy skills are important for three main reasons: First, in general, the financially literate congregant possesses the ability to apply basic financial knowledge to make informed decisions. Individuals that possess financial literacy skills are more capable of managing personal consumer debt. Financial literacy skills empower the individual to understand the ramifications of acquiring increased levels of debt. In addition, financial literacy skills provide an understanding of the importance of saving for the future – especially in the event of emergency. "Whether it is due to the stubbornness of entrenched behaviors, the release of pent-up consumer demand, or other factors, Americans are spending more, saving less, and still carrying credit card debt."[12]

Second, possessing financial literacy skills offers insight that allows individuals to avoid the pitfalls of predatory lending. Gallmeyer and Roberts (2009) noted that, "Payday lending serves as an indicator of economic distress within a community and contributes to the "poverty penalty" those populations endure and exacerbates their financial insecurity."[13] Financial insecurity often becomes a vicious cycle with mounting debt that becomes difficult to repay. "Check-cashing establishments, Payday loans and rent-to-own furniture businesses are also major contributors draining the pockets of low income people (Bullock, 2006)."[14] The interest rates and penalties generated by predatory loans can be quite exorbitant and extremely difficult to manage. Saunders et al., found, "Payday loans range from $100 to $1,000, depending on state legal maximum and annual

---

[11] AnnaMaria Lusardi and Olivia Mitchell, *The Economic Importance of Financial Literacy: Theory and Evidence* (Journal of Economic Literature, 2014).
[12] The 2011 Consumer Financial Literacy Survey Final Report, *National Foundation for Credit Counseling* (Harris Interaction Inc. Public Relations Group, 2011).
[13] Ibid.
[14] Lorinda Bullock, The High Cost of Being Poor, *Carolina Peacemaker* (Black Press Network, 2006). http://carolinapeacemaker.com accessed on September 17, 2012.

percentage rates run from 391% to 782% for a two-week extension of credit."[15] The recession in 2008-2009 coupled with high unemployment contributed to the loss of income for many individuals. A 2012 research study suggested, "Most borrowers use Payday loans to cover ordinary living expenses over the course of months, rather than unexpected emergencies over the course of weeks and the average borrower is indebted about five months of the year."[16] The average borrower of Payday loans seeks to fulfill basic needs and lacks sufficient income or an emergency savings account as a financial buffer for emergencies. High interest rates associated with predatory loans have become a great concern and cause many to be at risk for higher levels of indebtedness.

Gallmeyer and Roberts (2009) stated, "During the past decade there has been a rise in both economically distressed communities and predatory industries, which profit from them. Payday lending stands out for its rapid expansion in some communities, which provides high-interest loans in cash that can also trap borrowers in a spiral of debt."[17] McKernan and Ratcliffe (2008) asserted, "If low-income working families have too few assets to weather emergencies there is a tendency to utilize Payday loans, pawnbrokers, auto, and title loans with significant fees attached."[18] Individuals in lower income brackets often cannot afford the high costs associated with Payday loans and have few viable alternatives available to them. Gallmeyer and Roberts (2009) stated, "Minority communities are disproportionately exposed to the predatory lending industry. Historical racism and exclusion have placed minority groups, on average, in the lower tiers of the labor market and income ladder. Furthermore, continued discrimination and marginalization by traditional lending institutions,

---

[15] Lauren K. Saunders, Leah A. Plunkett, and Caroline Carter, *Stopping the Payday Loan Trap: Alternatives That Work, Ones That Don't* (National Consumer Law Center, 2010).

[16] Susan K. Urahn et al., *Pew Payday Lending in America: Who Borrows, Where They Borrow and Why* (The Pew Charitable Trusts, 2012).

[17] Alice Gallmeyer. and Wade T. Roberts, *Payday Lenders and Economically Distressed Communities: A Spatial Analysis of Financial Predation* (The Social Science Journal, 2009).

[18] Signe-Mary McKernan and Caroline Ratcliffe, *Enabling Families to Weather Emergencies and Develop the Role of Assets* (Urban Institute, New Safety Net Paper 7., 2008).

minority communities can be seen as vulnerable to the Payday loan industry."[19] Lusardi and Scheresburg (2013) found, "The alternative financial services (AFS) industry has experienced tremendous growth in the United States, particularly in the past twenty years."[20] The "unbanked" are persons that frequently utilize the alternate services industry and are not the only group who rely on non-banking services. Seidman and Kramer (2005) found, "The majority of the population that are banked still use non-bank services, ranging from purchasing money orders and sending remittances from nonbanks to using Payday lenders, pawnbrokers and auto title lenders as primary sources of credit."[21]

Third, financial literacy empowers individuals to seek relevant financial information and resources. The 2011 Consumer Financial Literacy Survey reported, "Credit card debt continues to present challenges for many Americans. As a result, two in three adults pay for most purchases with cash or debit cards, and two in five still carry credit card balances from month to month."[22] Making minimum credit card payments accompanied with high interest rates and penalties prolongs the debt repayment process. Lusardi and Scheresburg (2009) found, "Attitudes pertaining to poor personal fiscal management can be directly linked to consumer indebtedness."[23] Financial literacy skills can optimize financial decisions for the informed consumer and minimize the length of debt repayment and the total amount owed. Accumulating large amounts of credit card debt can be a hardship and difficult to repay unless individuals seek financial counseling from a reputable organization. In the 2011 Prudential Study respondents stated, "African Americans were more likely than the general population to indicate that reducing debt, improving credit-worthiness,

---

[19] Ibid.
[20] Annamaria Lusardi and Carlo De Bassa Scheresburg, *Financial Literacy and the High Cost of Borrowing in the United States* (National Bureau of Economic Research, FINRA Investor Education Foundation, 2013).
[21] Ellen Seidman, Moez Hababou, and Jennifer Kraemer, *Getting to Know the Unbanked Consumers: A Financial Services Analysis* (The Center for Financial Services Innovation, An Initiative of ShoreBank Advisory Services, 2005).
[22] Ibid.
[23] Annamaria Lusardi and Carlo De Bassa, *The Importance of Financial Literacy* (National Bureau of Economic Research Reporter: Research Summary, 2009).

and educating children about debt avoidance are critical or very important financial goals."[24]

It is important to recognize the African American community has enormous economic purchasing power that can be harnessed to transform their community. Rev. Soaries (2010) stated, "Considering the economic buying power of nearly $1 trillion annually, if African-Americans were a country, they would be the 16th largest country in the world."[25] Although the African American economic buying power is quite considerable, a wealth disparity continues to exist between Black and White households. Oliver and Shapiro (1997) noted, "A huge gap exists in the so-called comparative income-to-savings rate for whites and blacks, that is the rate at which each group places funds in savings accounts."[26] It is important for African Americans to build a savings reserve that directly correlates with their tremendous economic purchasing power. In 1997, Oliver and Shapiro reported, "Although African Americans as a whole possess a substantial amount of purchasing power, the level of savings and investment accounts are comparatively marginal."[27] Financial education and knowledge can be a motivating factor for African-American consumers to save and invest more of their incomes that can positively impact their churches, families and their communities.

Stewardship Efforts at First Agape Baptist Community of Faith

Since the founding of First Agape Baptist Community of Faith (FABCF) in 1999, the diaconate ministry at has conducted stewardship presentations during the Sunday morning worship service. In addition, stewardship principles as it pertains to tithes and offerings, are encouraged from the pulpit as the primary resource for the church. Although stewardship principles are taught on a consistent basis, several congregants

---

[24] Charles Lowrey and Sharon Taylor, *The African American Financial Experience* (The Prudential Research Study, Prudential Financial, Inc., 2011).
[25] National Newspapers Publishers' Association (NNPA), *State of the African American Consumer* (Black PressUSA, The Nielsen Company, 2011).
[26] Melvin L. Oliver and Thomas M. Shapiro, *Black Wealth/White Wealth – A New Perspective of Racial Inequality* (Routledge New York and London, 1997).
[27] Marvin L. Oliver and Thomas M. Shapiro, *Black Wealth and White Wealth: A New Perspective on Racial Inequality* (Routledge New York and London, 1997).

have expressed a concern, regarding personal consumer debt as a barrier to tithing. Many congregants have sought the diaconate, the pastor, and other church leaders to resolve their personal financial matters. As a result, the diaconate continues to provide individual financial counseling to congregants on an as needed basis. Unfortunately, many congregants have not utilized this resource in large measure. Since 1999, FABCF has provided substantial financial resources to congregants and local residents within Alexandria to alleviate personal financial hardships. Currently, FABCF no longer has the capacity to provide the level of financial resources it furnished in the past, which has become unsustainable.

Over the years, many tithers at FABCF have gone to be with the Lord. Furthermore, younger congregants have not filled this void to become tithers themselves. For a variety of reasons, fewer congregants are willing or able to tithe, although many have expressed a desire to do so. Congregants of all ages have shared their deepest concerns of feeling overwhelmed with consumer debt. Although a debt-free existence is not a prerequisite for tithing, the author has explored the financial barriers to tithing that surfaced based upon conversations with several congregants.

Background

Prior to the Great Recession of 2008-2009, African Americans' wealth was closely tied to the equity in their homes, which has decreased significantly since that time. Throughout the history of America, African Americans have experienced discrimination in employment, education, and housing opportunities. In 1998 Green stated, "Economics is one of the areas African Americans have faced the greatest racism."[28] In many cases, African Americans lost their homes due to foreclosures or experienced a loss of the equity in their homes as a result of "upside down mortgages" [where the market value of the home is less than the amount owed on the mortgage loan]. As a result, a recent Pew survey found that the net worth of African American households fell fifty-three percent due to the

---

[28] Kenneth Green, *Racism: It's Impact on the African American Family* (Leaven, Vol., 6, Issue 2, Article 9, 1998).

subprime mortgage crisis.[29] Undoubtedly, this is a cause for concern and the National Black Initiative responded by launching an historic savings program to address this economic disparity. "The National Black Church Initiative (NBCI), is a coalition of 34,000 churches that launched its Savings for Life Program. NBCI believes the church and its leaders have witnessed the destruction of Black families, Black communities and Black economic structures. NBCI initiated a plan to address the loss of wealth experienced by African Americans due to the economic recession as a result of deregulation in the banking and financial industry."[30]

The subprime mortgage crisis has triggered an investigation of the banking practices in the United States. Although it is rare for systemic irregularities to be revealed and corrected in a timely manner, "In May 2011, Wells Fargo settled a lawsuit in Memphis, Tennessee related to charges of discriminatory lending by awarding three million dollars for financial literacy."[31] Consequently, eight major banks were guilty of discriminating against African Americans in offering risky home loans. The Consumer Financial Protection Board (CFBP) Director Richard Cordray, said the findings showed that the bank's mortgage lending process "harmed the people who were overcharged or denied their dream of ownership based on their race." [32] Vanita Gupta, the head of the Department of Justice Civil Rights Division found discrimination based on race, which violated the civil rights laws and threatened the foundation of a fair economy.[33] In addition to discovering discriminatory banking practices, the mortgage crisis underscored the pervasiveness of low financial literacy and how it contributes to poor financial decisions. John Hope Bryant characterized the recent home mortgage crisis as a primary feature of financial illiteracy. Bryant stated, "At the heart of the economic crisis was a massive level

---

[29] Paul Taylor. et al., *Wealth Gaps Rise Between Whites, Blacks, and Hispanics* (Pew Research Center, Social and Demographic Trends, 2011).
[30] *The National Black Church Initiative* (National Black Church Initiative's Church-Based Small Business, 1991), accessed on July 19, 2014 www.naltblackchurch.com
[31] Mary Kane, *For Financial Literacy, A Surprising Political War* (Alica Patterson Foundation, 2012) http://aliciapatterson.org/stories/financial-literacy-surprising-political-war accessed on December 12, 2012.
[32] Kevin McCoy, *Bank to Pay 10.6M Over Loan Discrimination Charges*, USA TODAY, 2016.
[33] Ibid.

of borrower and consumer financial illiteracy and all-around greed of the banking industry"[34] The mortgage crisis in America was a poignant lesson in the importance of financial literacy that revealed mortgage holders naivety regarding their financial risk or financial vulnerability. As a result, African Americans experience financial hardships that often have an impact in the present and in the future.

In 2006, Operation HOPE founder John Hope Bryant stated, "Today, financial literacy is a civil rights issue, if you do not understand financial literacy, you're an economic slave."[35] The believer must integrate financial literacy skills with a focus on personal empowerment to become free from financial bondage. "The United States (U.S.) is one of the world's wealthiest nation and also has one of the largest gulfs between the rich and the poor. The top one percent of American families has more money (and wealth) than the bottom forty percent; this gap has steadily increased over the past seventy years."[36] The wealth gap has also contributed to the financial limitations that individuals face regarding saving and investing. In 2007, Karen Lincoln reported, "Older African Americans are particularly vulnerable to financial strain due to their disproportionate levels of poverty compared to Whites."[37] An accumulation of wealth - over a lifetime - as a resource for retirement is rare among African Americans, women and the poor. Low financial literacy is also linked to a lack of educational and employment opportunities for the aforementioned groups. Lusardi concluded, "Women display low debt literacy, and give themselves low ratings when assessing their own financial knowledge. In contrast, the elderly rank the lowest in terms of actual financial knowledge and this may explain the prevalence of financial scams perpetrated against the elderly.[38]

---

[34] John Hope Bryant, *Love Leadership: The New Way to Lead In a Fear-Based World* (Jossey-Bass, A Wiley Imprint, 2009).

[35] Michael A. Schwartz, *Martin Luther King's Atlanta Church Add Financial Literacy Training* (USA TODAY, 2010).

[36] Teresa Capra, *Poverty and It's Impact on Education: Today and Tomorrow, Thought and Action* (NEA Education Journal, 2009).

[37] Karen D. Lincoln, *Financial Strain; Negative Interactions: Personal Mastery, Pathways to Mental Health in Older African Americans* (Journal of Black Psychology, 2007).

[38] Ibid.

Historical Perspective

Reverend Richard Allen and Absalom Jones were forerunners of the mutual aid societies that promoted spiritual, social, and economic independence from Whites by "Free Negroes" known as the Free African Society (1746-1818).[39] Free African Societies sought independence from Whites and were an integral part of building churches and universities for African Americans to promote self-determination for the masses. Free people were comprised of: children born of free colored persons; mulatto children of white servants or free women; children of free Negro and Indian parents; and slaves who were set free.[40]

As the President of Virginia Seminary, Gregory W. Hayes recognized the ramifications of financial stewardship (circa 1890's). "Hayes was aware that Blacks had been very successful in building large and spacious houses of worship, and if the Negro was to succeed in building financial enterprises, s/he had to organize and operate from those ecclesiastical bases."[41] Historically, the church has been a resource to equip Blacks with skills, knowledge, and abilities that could be harnessed to improve their living standards. Since the Emancipation Proclamation by Abraham Lincoln on January 1, 1863, (became the 13th Amendment in December, 1865) financial empowerment has been fostered within the African American church. The African American church must continue to take a leadership role in this area to assist its congregants in the African American community to foster financial literacy.

African Americans have sought to achieve economic independence from Whites especially during the periods after the Emancipation Proclamation and during segregation in the United States. African Americans realized significant economic strides between 1865 and 1900.[42] Scott Ellsworth (1982) described three cities that were 'beacons of light' in what was

---

[39] Larry Brayboy, *The Black Church in America, - Preparing for a new Century* (Popular Truth Publishing, 2012).
[40] Ibid..
[41] Ralph Reavis, *Apostles of Self-Help and Interdependence: Chronicles of History* (Publishers Solutions, 2012).
[42] Lerone Bennett, Jr. *Before the Mayflower – A History of Black America* (Pengiun Books 6th Edition, 1993).

called 'Black Wall Street' prior to the Great Depression in 1929.[43] These cities were: Tulsa, Oklahoma; Richmond, Virginia; and Durham, North Carolina. In each instance, African American communities rallied together to build thriving economic and financial metropolises in the midst of harsh racial segregation and discriminatory practices, and became the envy of neighboring White communities.[44] Tulsa, Oklahoma experienced an economic decline based upon the deliberate undermining from the surrounding White community, which culminated during the Race Riot of 1921.[45] As a result of the race riot in Tulsa, Oklahoma the all-Black business district was destroyed and since that time has not resumed its prominence within the community.

When Blacks migrated to northern cities they often experienced discriminatory lending practices by local banks. To provide access to financial resources in Brooklyn, New York during the Great Migration (1916-1970), Rev. Dr. Gardner C. Taylor initiated a church-operated credit union. The credit union provided access to loans for African Americans when local banks failed to do so. Rev. Dr. Gardner C. Taylor led by example when he established a credit union as the pastor of Concord Baptist Church, which empowered his congregation in Bedford-Stuyvesant Brooklyn, New York in 1951. "The Concord Baptist Church Credit Union became a necessity based on the reaction of local banks that would not make loans to new African American migrants that arrived from the South."[46] As of October 2014, Concord Federal Credit Union had 1,346 members and over nine million dollars in assets![47]

An historical perspective suggests that the church first introduced views that African Americans possessed pertaining to money. Jakes (2000) stated, "Finance has for so long been a taboo subject among people of faith. The church taught African Americans that money was the root of all-evil

---

[43] Ellsworth Scott, *Death in a Promised Land* (Louisiana State University Press, 1982).
[44] Ibid.
[45] Ibid.
[46] *Concord Baptist Church of Christ*, Bedford Stuyvesant, Brooklyn, New York, accessed on June 25, 2014 http://www.concordcares.org/about-us/history
[47] National Credit Union Administration – www.ncua.gov

and should thus must be forsaken."[48] A misinterpretation of the scriptures is the belief that money is the root of all-evil and has been a widely accepted viewpoint among many African Americans for generations. A closer inspection of Timothy 6:10a states, "For the love of money is the root of all-evil."[49] Jakes (2000) noted, "The church and the Civil Rights Movement have championed many campaigns that opened employment and business opportunities for African Americans. However, after opening these doors, neither group has taught its followers what to do with their new sources of revenue."[50] Jakes (2009) noted, "For some, the focus on piety has caused them to lag behind."[51]

New trends to address to financial disparities in the African American community are beginning to surface. Schwartz (2010) reported, "The Ebenezer Baptist Church in Atlanta opened a financial literacy-training center to encourage its congregants to open savings accounts and to purchase their own homes."[52] These are the first steps in taking responsibility for the long-term financial needs of congregants by creating a more stable community through home ownership. Understanding financial products (i.e. saving, checking, and investment accounts and strategies) is also an important component of developing a spiritual and financial legacy for the African American family as a means of transferring wealth from one generation to the next.

Half-century later church leaders have recognized there have been missed opportunities to teach and to educate African American believers regarding their role and responsibility in Christian stewardship. In contrast, many African American pastors have promoted the *'prosperity gospel'*, which is considered controversial by many religious leaders. The *'prosperity gospel'* distorts the role of money in the lives of congregants. Rev. Soaries (2010) stated, "In light of today's weakened economy, perhaps the prosperity movement should consider focusing on financial literacy,

---

[48] T. D. Jakes. *The Great Investment – Faith, Family, and Finance* (G.P. Putnum's and Sons, 2000).
[49] 1 Timothy 6:10a
[50] Ibid.
[51] Ibid.
[52] Michael A. Schwartz, *Martin Luther King's Atlanta Church Adds Financial Literacy Training* (USA TODAY 2010).

personal discipline, and saving for the long term."[53] Today, the challenge is to redirect the masses and to teach believers a new way of thinking about their personal finances. "Churches can be effective in teaching their congregants how to convert from a culture of borrowing and spending to a culture of saving and investing."[54]

Overview of Resources In Alexandria

Identifiable Challenges In The Local Ministry

There are several identifiable challenges in the City of Alexandria, Virginia. Many of the challenges involve the economic and educational status of African Americans that live at or near the poverty level. As the effects of the economic recession of 2008-2009 lingers, individuals that are gainfully employed are less likely to donate to community service organizations. As a result, a limited pool of resources must be shared among a larger group of people.[55]

The first challenge is the rising cost of higher education, which directly impacts the ability for an individual to finish college or a professional training program without incurring large amounts of debt. The decision to attend a two-year college or a technical training school may substantially reduce the amount of long-term debt one might incur at a private four-year college or state university. A notable disparity now exists based on a regulation that the U.S. Congress passed in 2013 to increase the interest rates for government student loans offered to the public, while maintaining the previous loan rate structure, for Congress members' children and federal workers.[56]

The second challenge is the lack of affordable housing in Alexandria, Virginia. The City of Alexandria's long-range strategic plans have displaced

---

[53] DeForest B. Soaries, *Black Churches and the Prosperity Gospel: Depending on Miracles as a Financial Strategy is a Dangerous Way to Live*, 2010, Wall Street Journal online assessed on November 20, 2012 http://online.wsj.com/article/SB10001424052748704116004575522202425314706.html

[54] Ibid.

[55] Ibid.

[56] Paul Singer, *Taxpayers Pay Millions for Federal Workers' Student Loans*, USA TODAY, 2013

many low-income families in recent years. Many residents have relocated to nearby jurisdictions within the Washington, D.C Metropolitan Area seeking affordable housing. Renters living within the City of Alexandria often reside in subsidized housing that is slowing disappearing and rental costs that often claims a higher percentage of the renters' monthly income.

The third challenge is to empower congregants to manage their modest incomes in a metropolitan area with a relatively high cost of living. The convergence of the economic recession, high unemployment, underemployment, and stagnant salaries contributes to mounting personal financial debt. As a result of the high cost of living and low or stagnant wages, individuals fall further behind financially when there are fewer opportunities for economic advancement without marketable employment skills.

Financial literacy affects the social, economic, political, academic, and spiritual life of the African American congregant. The mission of the church is to address the needs of congregants that extend beyond Sunday morning worship services. The main objective is to restore the original intent of stewardship as a biblical model that will benefit the congregant in every facet of their lives.

Academic literacy has an important relationship to financial literacy as it includes the ability to read and comprehend complex information. Academic literacy in America is an important issue that has been debated for several decades. "The importance of education should not be underestimated as many studies have shown there is a direct correlation between wealth and education, even after controlling for permanent income."[57] As individuals become more educated they are often exposed to an environment that introduces key financial concepts. In 2014, Cole, Paulson, and Shastry reported, "Academic pursuits that involve critical thinking and mathematical concepts ultimately determine the

---

[57] Annamaria Lusardi. *Financial Education and the Saving Behavior of African-American and Hispanic Households.* (Department of Economics Dartmouth College Hanover, New Hampshire. September 2005).

financial acumen one is likely to acquire."[58] Cole et al., (2014) found, "There was a strong correlation between mandated math courses and comprehension of financial concepts. Mathematics courses may provide the fundamental knowledge necessary to attain financial literacy skills and suggests significant exposure to math courses correlates with higher levels of financial literacy.[59]

Political literacy is also related to financial literacy and has long-term consequences for the Black church. Political literacy involves understanding issues that affect the community and the public policies that influence every facet of daily life. National and state legislators pass legislation, which influence tax policies, banking regulations and educational standards that mandate financial literacy programs in the schools and in the workplace. An argument used to rally support for the lottery and local casino establishments has less than favorable outcomes for the financial health of its citizens. A study by Stanley and French (2003) found, "In Florida, the educational system has received billions of lottery proceeds and the state legislature have taken lottery monies previously designated for education to fund other state commitments."[60] Subsequently, the number of financial literacy programs in the schools have been reduced or eliminated due to state and local budget shortfalls. Citizens are often encouraged to support the casino industry as a resource primarily for educational purposes for grades K-12. Typically, tax revenues are set aside for educational purposes are often redistributed elsewhere and abandons the initial goal to provide financial literacy to the community it serves. The redistribution of tax revenues for educational purposes is poorly understood within the community. The redistribution of tax revenues is rarely publicized in the media and communities are often unaware of how tax revenues are being utilized.

Understandably, socioeconomic, political, and cultural mores have

---

[58] Shawn Cole Anna Paulson, and Gauri Kartini Shastry. *High School Curriculum and Financial Outcomes: The Impact of Mandated Personal Finance and Mathematical Courses.* Harvard Business School Working Paper, No. 13-064, January 2013. (Revised April 2014.)

[59] Ibid.

[60] Rodney E. Stanley and Edward P. French, *Can Students Truly Benefit From State Lotteries: A Look At Lottery Expenditures Towards Education in the American States*, (The Social Science Journal, 2003), 40.

shaped how money is viewed in the African American community. High rates of unemployment, underemployment, and the lack of educational opportunities have an impact on an individual's ability to save, invest, purchase a home, retire, or to build and transfer wealth to the next generation. In order for the community to thrive, it is important to develop methods to educate the African American community on how to adapt to changes in the economic and political structures as they change within the United States.

Finally, a key requirement to improve financial literacy, academic literacy, and political literacy is the pursuit of a college education, specialized technical training, and entrepreneurship. Harris (2010) found, "An increase in earning power for African American professionals and entrepreneurs is often based on additional levels of education."[61] Academic literacy and political literacy are also likely to increase political activism in the African American community related to the local and national legislative issues that affect daily their living.

To the degree which financial literacy skills are developed, refined, and implemented may determine the financial future for many congregants. Lusardi and Scheresburg (2013) noted, "As with financial illiteracy, debt illiteracy is particularly severe among the elderly, the young, women, minorities, and individual that are divorced or separated."[62] Financial literacy also includes familiarity with basic banking and financial products.

In a (May 2014) webinar sponsored by the National Urban League, Jacquette M. Timmons, a financial behaviorist emphasized, "As an individual considers him or herself a *'chief executive officer'* (CEO) or a key financial decision maker within the family unit they become more effective in making informed financial decisions."[63] A CEO makes financial decisions based upon their strengths, weaknesses, opportunities,

---

[61] Angel L. Harris, *The Economic and Educational State of Black Americans in the 21st Century: Should We Be Optimistic or Concerned?* (The Review of Black Political Economy, 2010).

[62] Annamaria Lusardi and Carlo de Bassa Scheresburg, *Financial Literacy and the High-Cost of Borrowing in the United States,* (National Bureau of Economic Research, 2013).

[63] Jacquette M. Timmons, *Your Money and Your Career,* a webinar sponsored by the National Urban League, held on May 6, 2014 www.jacquettetimmons.com/make-money-pleasurable

and threats (SWOT) of their business (or personal finances). These assessments are a means to fortify and develop a strategy for success. The CEO or head of the household is purposeful and focused on seeking resources to make informed financial decisions. The CEO/head of the household is a learner who networks with subject matter experts that can provide greater insight to the financial barriers they may face.[64] Ms. Timmons described the "financial wheel" as an interdependent assessment pertaining to what an individual will earn, spend, save and invest. This model describes the interdependency between each category as it affects the life of the individual. Individuals must be proactive rather than reactive to address - income that is earned, saved and invested - rather than reacting to circumstances that may arise in the event of an emergency.[65] (Appendix B)

Financial experts recommend researching a topic at hand or "doing their homework" to evaluate the merits of a personal financial decision to mitigate negative outcomes leading to indebtedness. Savings are a crucial financial management tool utilized to weather emergencies. Financial shocks such as car repairs, loss of employment, and health care expenses can be remedied through a robust savings account. Wolf (2012) described, "The role of assets and debts enables low-income families to cope with financial emergenices."[66] When low-income families have limited resources they may be faced with few options in the event of an emergency. The absence of a robust savings account in an emergency makes the individual more vulnerable to financial debt and costly financial mistakes.

In addition, deregulation has created an environment that has removed long held legal protections and an infrastructure with an important 'check and balance system' used to promote stability in the financial markets. As the banking industry loosened its restrictions on home mortgage loans many banks simultaneously secured loans for more risky mortgage holders. This banking practice ultimately became unsustainable and the economic ramifications became costly to both the American and global economies.[67]

Friedman (2005) indicated, "Financial literacy programs are more

---

[64] Ibid.
[65] Ibid.
[66] Edward N. Wolf, *Enabling Families to Weather Emergencies and Develop* (The Urban Institite, 2012), accessed on June 11, 2014 at http://www.urban.org
[67] Ibid.

likely to keep participants engaged and complete important skills training if specific needs are addressed such as first-time homebuyers and mortgage lending."[68] Unless individuals are enrolled in first time homebuyer programs, it is unlikely financial literacy skills, will be offered within their communities. As various types of financial literacy programs are examined more closely, it appears that faith-based financial literacy programs, are rare entities that occur at a rate of only nine percent.[69] (Appendix C) The church must utilize this opportunity to equip congregants and to fill the void by providing opportunities to acquire basic financial literacy skills.

Financial literacy programs target grades K-12 and college students are on the rise and there are several nationwide initiatives that have been established: "Jump$tart, a coalition for personal financial literacy in the schools, is a partnership of approximately one hundred fifty organizations and entities from the corporate, non-profit, academic, government [sectors] that have been adopted by the state of Virginia."[70] The Virginia Department of Education added financial literacy skills training to grades K-12 in the academic curriculum. In May 2010, the goal of the Jump$tart resource guide was to inspire leaders at all levels to develop partnerships and create financial capability initiatives as a means to improve the financial well being of every American.

An initiative was established by President Barack Obama's administration to address financial literacy in the United States. "The President's Advisory Council on Financial Capability was created on January 29, 2010, by Executive Order by President Barack Obama and Jack Lew, Secretary of the Treasury provided ways to empower Americans to improve their financial capability."[71] The Executive Order addressed gaps between financial capabilities versus low financial literacy as a national response to improve the financial well being of Americans based on the

---

[68] Pamela Friedman, *Providing and Funding Financial Literacy Programs for Low-Income Adults and Youth* (The Finance Project, 2005).

[69] Vitt et al., *Personal Finance and the Rush to Competence: Financial Literacy Education in the U.S.* (Fannie Mae Foundation, and Institute for Socio-Financial Studies, 2001).

[70] Jump$tart Coalition for Personal Literacy, *Personal Financial Survey of High School Seniors*: Executive Summary. (Coalition for Personal Literacy, 2004).

[71] Executive Order 13530 - *President's Advisory Council on Financial Capability*, January 29, 2010.

most current research and economic trends. Lerman and Bell (2006) observed, "In recognizing the importance of financial decisions, a number of public agencies, private foundations, school systems, and employers have begun to sponsor financial literacy programs."[72]

The need for financial literacy education is clear and may be more acute in minority communities. Lusardi (2013) found, "The effects of financial education on saving and investment behavior have gained precedence over recent years and few have focused on minority groups. Understanding the saving and investment behaviors of African-Americans and Hispanics is critically important for devising and implementing policies that can be effective in shaping the behavior of families where savings are most scarce.[73] A survey by Lusardi (2009) found, "A stark contrast in measuring actual knowledge. The majority of individuals gave themselves high knowledge ratings, pointing to a gulf between how much people actually know and how much they think they know."[74] The difference in what individuals know and what they think they know is quite stark.

Financial literacy programs can also be instrumental to support the financial interests of congregants and the church to provide important services to the community. "The one who increases his wealth by increasing interest gathers it for someone who is gracious to the needy. Proverbs 28:8."[75] Examples of economic inequities that adversely affect African Americans are prevalent throughout our society and must be addressed. For instance, the bank lender negotiates the interest rate a homebuyer will pay based on their credit worthiness. Nevertheless, those who can least afford high mortgage interest rates are often required to pay more than their moderate-income counterparts. In 2006, an article in the Carolina Peacemaker, entitled the "High Cost of Being Poor" on average, low-income homeowners (30K or less) paid interest rates as high as nearly

---

[72] Robert I. Lerman and Elizabeth Bell, *Financial Literacy Strategies: Where Do We Go From Here?* (Opportunity and Ownership Project, Report No.1, The Urban Institute, 2006).

[73] Ibid.

[74] Annamaria Lusardi, *The Importance of Financial Literacy*, (National Bureau of Economic Research, NBER Reporter: Research Summary 2009), Number 2, www.nber.org/reporter/2009number2/lusardi.htm assessed on September 12, 2012.

[75] Proverbs 28:8

seven percent, while adults with incomes higher than $120K paid a rate of five percent.[76]

It is a startling fact that many low-income households are more likely to utilize the lottery to attain household wealth. In a recent consumer study by the Brookings Institute, "Twenty-one percent of adults surveyed – including thirty-eight percent of those with incomes below $25,000 – reported that winning the lottery was the most practical strategy for accumulating several hundred thousand dollars of wealth for their retirement."[77] Notably, there are investment opportunities that consumers can utilize to achieve their personal savings and retirement goals that are less risky and provide a greater return on their investment over the long term. Friedman et al., stated, "It is a misnomer to believe that the majority of low-income families cannot save and do not save."[78] Low-income families can restructure their financial outlook and reverse their indebtedness and begin to build a savings reserve. "Years of rigorous research by experts at the Urban Institute and the Corporation for Enterprise Development (CFED), has shown that despite very low incomes, a substantial portion (44 percent) of these households accumulated enough to escape asset poverty in twelve years."[79]

Special Insights Regarding The Problem Area

There are special insights to shed light on the barriers that exist to promote and to improve financial literacy. Webb and Sheeran (2006) supported the idea that, "Changing human behavior requires the individual to have a desire to modify negative financial behaviors."[80] There must also be an impetus to engage adults that seek to change their long held financial behaviors, long-standing myths, and biases. As with any behavior change there must be a sincere desire to empower adults who possess low financial literacy skills. An individual must recognize the

---

[76] Ibid.
[77] William G. Gale and Ruth Levine, *Financial Literacy: What Works? How Could It Be More Effective?* (Urban-Brookings Tax policy Center, Brookings Institute, 2010).
[78] Bob Friedman, Ying Shi and Sarah R. Wartell, *Savings: The Poor Can Save, Too*, Democracy: A (Journal of Ideas, Issue #26, 2012).
[79] Ibid.
[80] Thomas L. Webb and Paschal Sheeran (Psychological Bulletin, Vol. 132, 2006), 2.

need to make adjustments in the most extreme cases to avoid or recover from bankruptcy. The Personal Financial Literacy Management Course acknowledged, "No one ever sets out to declare bankruptcy, and according to the Administrative Office of the U.S. Courts, 1,412,838 households filed for bankruptcy in 2009."[81] As a result, when bankruptcy occurs, the credit reporting agencies will continue to list a bankruptcy for at least seven to ten years. Bankruptcy poses significant barriers to re-establishing good credit. Skiba and Tobacman (2007) found, "Although the average size of the typical Payday loan is only $300, the loan approval for first-time applicants increased the two-year Chapter 13 bankruptcy filing rate by 2.48 percentage points."[82]

The need to make financial information and educational tools available to congregants can make a difference for individuals with low to moderate incomes. Bell and Lerman (2005) reported, "Low-income families are especially vulnerable to misinformation."[83] Furthermore, there are few models of financial education available to the public except for first time home-buying programs.

Consequently, managing debt and building wealth is a challenge unless financial interventions are made available to congregants. Lerman and Bell (2005) stated, "Unless incentives to save and invest are strong, many low-and-moderate-income families often lack the basic knowledge to manage income wisely, build wealth, and avoid excessive debt."[84] As previously stated, state lotteries are considered by many as a viable method to build personal wealth. Long-term savings and investment strategies are much more effective and impose fewer financial risks.

Incentives such as employer matching contributions through 401k retirement programs are often successful regardless of economic downturns. Gale and Levine (2010) found, "Although efforts at raising awareness about financial literacy have been met with at best mixed success, there are

---

[81] Personal Financial Management Course, Your Start to a Fresh Financial Future, 2010, accessed onSeptember 20, 2012 www.DebtorEdu.com.
[82] Paige Marta Skiba and Jeremy Tobacman, *Do Payday Loans Cause Bankruptcy?*(Horowitz Foundation and the Harvard Economics Department, 2007).
[83] Robert I. Lerman and Elizabeth Bell, *Can Financial Literacy Enhance Asset Building?* Opportunity and Ownership Project. (The Urban Institute. No. 6, 2005).
[84] Ibid.

private actions and public strategies that can influence saving behavior."[85] These include, but are not limited to, the Association of African American Financial Advisors (AAAFA), which partners with the Fannie Mae Foundation, Prince George's Community College, Reid Community Development Corporation, First Combined Community Federal Credit Union and the Literacy Institute for Financial Enrichment.[86]

In comparison to other persons of color (Hispanics and Asians) African Americans were least likely to have a savings account. According to Duong et al., (2014) reported, "Five percent of African Americans, eight percent of Hispanics and eleven percent of Asian American and Pacific Islanders (AAPI) have a savings account'[87] Checking accounts were more likely to be used instead of a savings account by persons of color. Between 2007-2009, for AAPI the rate of checking accounts was thirty-two percent, for Hispanics it was thirty-one percent, and for African Americans it was twenty-four percent.[88] African Americans remain the largest minority group in the United States, however their size in proportion did not correlate with their use of banking services such as saving, checking, and investment accounts.

---

[85] Ibid.
[86] American Association of African American Financial Advisors (AAAA).
[87] Jane Duong, Alvina Condon, Katie Taylor, Marisabel Torres, Lindsay Daniels et al., *Banking In Color: New Findings on Financial Access for Low and Moderate Income Communities,* (The National Coalition for Asian Pacific American Community Development, National Urban League, and La Raza, 2014).
[88] Ibid.

CHAPTER TWO

The State of The Art In This Ministry Model

Researchers, economists, politicians, and clergy have identified financial literacy skills as a national concern that disproportionally affects African Americans, women, young adults, the elderly, and the poor. The state of the art ministry model and literature review includes financial literacy research. The four basic financial literacy training methods that can be found primarily within the United States are: 1) Asset building for low-income families with matching savings accounts; 2) Asset building for low-income families without savings accounts; 3) Assessment of psychological readiness/behavior change; 4) Value-centered decision-making financial literacy programs.

Financial literacy is described as an important life skill to have in the 21st century and has significant implications for the economic future of African Americans. As Vitt succinctly explains it, the need for financial literacy education is growing in importance in all sectors of the United States largely in response to public initiatives that call on Americans to save and invest for long-term financial independence. Concerns about the long-term solvency of Social Security, and shifts in responsibility from the government to citizens and from employers to employees are drivers alerting individuals and families to bleak future prospects without an accumulation of adequate monetary resources for later life. (Vitt, 2001) [89]

Financial literacy is a concern as it relates to the solvency of the Social Security system. Increasingly, citizens rely on government resources to supplement income during their retirement years. In "A Rush to Competency," Vitt et al., (2001) determined that a lack of attention to this important issue has negative repercussions in the lives of individuals, families, and the American economy.[90] More important, few individuals save for their retirement and often carry high levels of credit card and student loan debt. During the mortgage crisis, the entire economic landscape was adversely affected and few Americans were left unscathed. A 2011 Prudential study found, "African Americans are less knowledgeable about asset accumulation and financial asset protection products, and consequently have low levels of ownership of Individual Retirement Accounts (IRAs), stocks and bonds, mutual funds, and annuities."[91] Understandably, financial concepts can be a challenge for many to acquire unless there is deliberate attempt to obtain and practice these financial literacy skills. Kunkler (2013) stated, "The more financial reference points an individual has the more accurate and precise their decision-making will become on the fuzzy subject of finance."[92]

In 2010, an Executive Order (EO) was signed by President Barack Obama to create the President's Advisory Council on Financial Capability, which recognized financial literacy as an important issue that is relevant to the operation of the country.[93] Financial capability among Americans will continue to be monitored closely to drive future policies that will make necessary adjustments to promote the financial success of its citizens within

---

[89] Vitt et al., *Personal Finance and the Rush to Competence: Financial Literacy Education in the U.S.* (Fannie Mae Foundation, and Institute for Socio-Financial Studies, 2001).
[90] Ibid.
[91] Charles Lowrey and Sharon Taylor, *The African American Experience* (Prudential Research, Prudential Financial, Inc., 2011).
[92] Duke Kunkler, *Financial Literacy – Timeless Concepts to Turn Financial Chaos into Clarity* (Kunkler, 2012).
[93] Ibid.

the U.S. "The President has established a Council to review, research, and address financial matters that contribute to the financial stability of the Federal Government, to promote, and to enhance financial capability among the American people."[94] In collaboration with the Department of Treasury, the Education Commission, and the President's Advisory Council designed strategies to improve financial education in every segment of society. To this end, the Presidential Executive Order will remain active for two consecutive years (2012) and will be extended based upon recommendations to the President that warrant an extension and is funded through an appropriated budget process. The 2012, National Financial Capability Study, written by the Financial Industry Regulatory Authority (FINRA), identified the root cause of financial illiteracy and possible solutions. FINRA found, "Americans are experiencing difficulty with making ends meet, planning ahead, and managing financial products."[95] The population of low investors (low-income) disproportionately experience financial strains in every category measured.

Literature Review

In the first category, making ends meet – nineteen percent of individuals surveyed are spending more than their income and twenty-six percent have medical bills that are over due.[96] As a result, individuals may become more reliant on credit cards, Payday or Title loans to augment their income and subsequently credit scores decline and personal debt rises, which alters personal financial stability and prolongs financial hardship.

Second, fifty-six percent of individuals do not have an emergency savings or a 'rainy day' fund. It is recommended that households save at least three months of living expenses in the event of an emergency.[97] As individuals find it difficult to make ends meet, saving for emergencies becomes a tremendous strain. A vicious cycle may persist where regular borrowing may occur without the ability to repay the debt. Lastly,

---

[94] Ibid.
[95] Gerri Walsh et al., *National Financial Capability Study* (Financial Industry Regulatory Authority, 2013).
[96] Ibid.
[97] Ibid. 36.

managing financial products can become a complicated issue especially when an individual utilizes nonbanking institutions (alternative finance services – such as check cashing establishments) that do not customarily provide financial education or training.

A wealth disparity exists between Blacks and Whites based on a recent survey. In 1997, Oliver and Shapiro reported, "previous studies comparing the wealth of Blacks and Whites found that Blacks have anywhere from $8 to $19 of wealth for every $100 that Whites possess."[98] The income gap that exists between Blacks and Whites only partly explains the reasons for income disparity and research supports other issues such as a comparatively low level of savings and investments.

Gallmeyer and Roberts reported, "African-Americans and Hispanics also have lower financial literacy than Whites, which correlates with poor savings and investment behavior."[99] Furthermore, African Americans are less likely to invest in stocks and bonds, IRA's, and annuities even at moderate-income levels. Gallmeyer and Roberts (2009) found, "Minorities may generally have a mistrust of investing in equity markets or perceive discrimination and self-select away from formal financial institutions where they feel discriminated against. African Americans are also likely to face means-tested programs that discourage asset possession such as Medicare or Medicaid programs."[100]

Purchasing a home is less likely to occur among African Americans in comparison to Whites and may be the best method to transfer wealth from one generation to the next. Oliver and Shapiro (1997) stated, "Blacks owned only three percent of all accumulated wealth in the United States in 1984, even though they received 7.6% of the total money earned that year and made up eleven percent of all households."[101] These statistics demonstrate the disparities that are prevalent based on every financial indicator except for purchasing power. A 2011 Nielsen findings substantiated, "African

---

[98] Melvin L. Oliver and Thomas M. Shapiro, *Black Wealth/White Wealth – A New Perspective on Racial Inequality,* Routledge New York and London, 1997.
[99] Alice Gallmeyer. and Wade T. Roberts, *Payday Lenders and Economically Distressed Communities: A Spatial Analysis of Financial Predation* (The Social Science Journal, 2009).
[100] Ibid.
[101] Ibid.

American buying power of one trillion annually is projected to climb to 1.1 trillion by 2015."[102] Large companies frequently possess sophisticated marketing strategies to study and target African Americans and others based upon their buying habits. The impetus must be to redirect the financial resources African Americans possess to promote saving and investing for the future. It is noteworthy, that the buying power of African Americans is rarely mentioned in business news other than reporting from the Black Press.

Operation HOPE (John Bryant Hope) commissioned a survey by (Mandell) through the Jump$tart program to measure the level of financial literacy in high school seniors. Mandell (2011) wrote, "In contrast to young White adults, African-Americans of the same age have lower levels of financial literacy and the trend is not improving. This deficiency is true for all income levels, with relative scores decreasing for African-Americans with higher family incomes. The data seems to indicate that young African-Americans place relatively more emphasis on spending than on saving. While this is true of Americans in general, it appears to be somewhat more pronounced among African-Americans."[103] In 2004, the survey results demonstrated "Eighty percent of White students scored a grade of "C" or better (seventy-five percent correct), less than one percent of African-American students did so. At the other extreme, 86.4 percent of African-American students "failed" the exam (less than sixty percent correct) compared to 57.8 percent of White students."[104] The data clearly demonstrated a marked deficiency in financial knowledge among African-American young adults who often do not receive financial literacy training at school or in the home. Soaries (1996) stated, "A practical strategy is to identify false beliefs, inconsistent values, and harmful habits that have kept African Americans locked in comfortable consumer prisons."[105] The

---

[102] National Newspapers Publisher's Association, *State of the African American Consumer* (Black PressUSA, Nielsen Company, 2011).

[103] Lewis Mandell, *State of Financial Literacy of Young African-American Adults in America,* Special Report Commissioned by Operation HOPE, Inc. (State University of New York at Buffalo and the Jump$tart Coalition for Personal Financial Literacy Based Upon a Survey (Sponsored by Merrill-Lynch, 2004).

[104] Ibid.

[105] Deforest D. Soaries Jr., *dfree Breaking Free from Finanical Slavery,* (Zondervon Publishers, 2011).

basis for correcting erroneous knowledge is to eradicate current financial practices and to acquire new skills to make informed financial decisions. Lusardi and Mitchell (2014) found, "Financial knowledge impacts key outcomes, including borrowing, saving, and investing decisions, not only during the worklife, but afterwards, in retirement, as well."[106]

First, the financial training method that is utilized in financial literacy programs includes Individual Development Accounts (IDA's). IDA's were once popular programs with matching saving accounts and declined due to the economic downturn in 2008 -2009. Friedman (2012) et al., "Determined utilizing matching savings accounts such as Individual Development Accounts (IDAs) was effective for low-income savers."[107] IDA's typically matched two to one for individuals enrolled in the program. Another feature of IDA programs included stimulating job creation and self-employment for individuals within the program. Matching savings accounts were a key element to assist individuals in curbing the use of costly financial products such as check-cashing establishments.

The second financial literacy training method is asset building. In 2005, Bell and Lerman agreed, "Asset building reduces excessive debt, however more efforts are needed to improve financial decisions over the long-term."[108] Asset building programs may only meet short-term goals for many participants, leaving many to return to past practices. Families at lower income levels typically save at slower rates and accumulate fewer assets in comparison to higher income families. McKernan and Racliffe (2008) claimed, "If low-income working families have too few assets to weather emergencies, they often turn to pay-day lenders and pawn brokers for temporary cash shortages."[109] Creditworthiness is also a concern for the unbanked consumer as their source of acquiring cash quickly is

---

[106] Annamarie Lusardi and Oliva Mitchell, *The Economic Importance of Financial Literacy: Theory and Evidence* (Journal of Economic Literature, 2014).

[107] Bob Friedman, Ying Shi and Sarah Rosen Wartell, *Savings: The Poor Can Save, Too, Democracy: A Journal of Ideas*, Issue #26) http://www.democracyjournal.org/26/savings-the-poor-can-save-too.php accessed on September 17, 2012.

[108] Elizabeth Bell and Robert I. Lerman, *Can Financial Literacy Enhance Asset Building?* Opportunity and Ownership Project (The Urban Institute, 2005).

[109] Signe-Mary McKernan and Caroline Ratcliffe, *Enabling Families to Weather Emergencies and Develop:The Role of Assets* (The Urban Institute, New Safety Paper 7, 2008).

compromised. Encouraging asset building to weather financial emergencies is an important tool to avoid the use of non-bank establishments that have proven to be very costly. In a 2012 article by Friedman et al., "There was a consensus that families with lower incomes do save. However, many assets were reduced significantly when many low income homeowners lost their homes due to the sub-prime mortgages crisis."[110] Independent of the financial crisis, studies have shown that low-income families are more likely to save than once thought. McKernan (2012) et al., reported, "Families above and below the poverty line were able to accrue more assets although at comparatively smaller amounts."[111] The smaller levels of savings can wither away in an emergency. Lusardi (2004) found, "Asset building is particularly important for the least wealthy groups which includes women, African Americans, Hispanics, and the elderly. Attending seminars appears to increase financial wealth by approximately eighteen percent."[112] There is a consensus that asset building is a useful tool for low-income families.

In 2006, Michele Singletary emphasized, "The importance of asset building using a values-based model, which includes saving and teaching children how to save at an early age"[113] Many are living above their means and must seek ways to save for large purchases or *'wants'*. Saving for important purchases builds discipline, self-sacrifice, and planning to avoid self-indulgence. Singletary is a firm believer of meeting basic needs first and to delay wants and desires that are often mistaken as *'needs'*.

The third financial literacy training method is theory-based or a behavior modification program. Xiao (2001) et al., indicated, "It is fruitful to develop and offer theory-based financial education programs that have affected participants' financial behavior, especially those using the experiential change processes such as consciousness raising. In future program designs, educators could have a greater impact on the

---

[110] Ibid., 39.

[111] Signe-Mary McKernan, Caroline Ratcliffe and Tina W. Shanks, *Can the Poor Accumulate Assets?* Opportunity and Ownership Facts (The Urban Institute, 2012).

[112] Annamaria Lusardi, *Saving and the Effectiveness of Financial Education*, In Pension Design and Structure: New Lessons from Behavioral Finance (Edited by Olivia Mitchell and Stephen Utkus, New York: Oxford University Press, 2004).

[113] Michelle Singletary, *Your Money and Your Man – How You and Prince Charming Can Spend Well and Live Rich* (Random House, 2006).

behavior change."[114] Still an important component of behavior change in the psychology model measures an individual's readiness to change. If an individual has been identified as '*not ready to change*' based upon a survey instrument or an interview, it is recommended that intervention be delayed until such time the individual is ready. Xiao (2001) et al., noted, "Since 1997, the Transtheoretical model (TTM) of change continues to be a revolution in the science of behavior. Traditional action paradigms generally focus on changes that progress slowly. TTM has shown through twenty years of research that behavior change is a process, not an event."[115] TTM includes the following processes:

This construct refers to the temporal dimension of behavioral change. In the transtheoretical model, change is a "process involving progress through a series of stages"

- Precontemplation ("not ready") – "People are not intending to take action in the foreseeable future, and can be unaware that their behavior is problematic"
- Contemplation ("getting ready") – "People are beginning to recognize that their behavior is problematic, and start to look at the pros and cons of their continued actions"
- Preparation ("ready") – "People are intending to take action in the immediate future, and may begin taking small steps toward behavior change"
- Action – "People have made specific overt modifications in modifying their problem behavior or in acquiring new healthy behaviors"
- Maintenance – "People have been able to sustain action for at least six months and are working to prevent relapse"
- Termination – "Individuals have zero temptation and they are sure they will not return to their old unhealthy habit as a way of coping"

---

[114] Jing J. Xiao et al., *Application of the Transtheoretical Model of Change To Financial Behavior*, (Consumer Interests Annual Volume 47, 2001).
[115] Ibid.

Financial literacy coupled with adult education is recommended to modify behavior and to optimize program outcomes. Forte et al., (2014) stated, "Adult financial literacy education works best in a theory-based framework that offers an evaluation component to measure programmatic success."[116]

David Ramsey identifies financial behavior as eighty percent of the personal money management process and only twenty percent financial knowledge.[117] Addressing and modifying the behaviors that are linked to poor money management (and or practices) is a key component. It is especially important to recognize spending as it becomes a reflection of one's self-esteem, self worth, or trying to measuring up to a false image, which is dangerous. Ramsey promotes the need to develop healthy financial habits that will transform individual lives.

The fourth financial literacy training method is a value-based program. Vitt (2009) suggested, "Personal values are the key to making decisions regarding monetary choices. We all make our decisions on the basis of: internal, social, physical and financial values."[118] Personal values also include a family history of managing financial matters, formal education, and religious beliefs that influence financial decisions and preferences. Financial literacy experts suggest that financial expenditures are value-based and are driven by issues that are not necessarily related to money, such as social expectations, peer pressure, and the impact materialism has on the individual(s). Vitt (2009) found, "Financial literacy training in a community-based or religious-based setting is more likely to be successful as it is considered a more relaxed atmosphere."[119] Most important, behavior change can occur by reshaping the participants' values based upon social and cultural influences. (Appendix D) Jecewiz (2013) stated that, "Maslow's Hierarchy of Needs is characterized as the following:

---

[116] Karin Sprow Forte et al., *New Directions for Adult and Continuing Education - Financial Literacy and Adult Education* (Number 141, Jossey-Bass., 2014).
[117] David Ramsey. *The Total Money Makeover: Classic Edition: A Proven Plan forFinancial Fitness* (Thomas Nelson Publishers, 2013).
[118] Lois Vitt, *Values-Centered Financial Education Understanding Cultural Influences on Learners' Financial Behaviors* (The Institute for Socio-Financial Studies and the National Endowment for Financial Education, 2009).
[119] Ibid.

1. Physiological and Safety Needs;
2. Belonging and Esteem Needs and;
3. Self-Actualization (the pinnacle of self fulfillment).

It is understood that money fulfills a need that provides a sense of security for the individual. Consequently, financial literacy is extremely important."[120] To put it simply, if an individual is concerned about fulfilling basic human needs such as food, safety, shelter, and clothing – it is less likely s/he is able to focus on self-actualization, or personal growth and development as it pertains to financial literacy. (Appendix E)

In a faith-based setting, stewardship principles can be taught to individuals regarding the scriptural basis for tithing, *'giving back'*, and using resources effectively by sharing with the less fortunate. Vitt et al., (2000) found, "Financial attitudes are deeply embedded in the literature of most religions. Many western financial behaviors stem from the Judeo-Christian traditions and laws laid down in the Old and New Testaments of the bible."[121] Faith-based financial literacy programs re-enforce stewardship principles that include but are not limited to tithing, debt management; borrowing and lending; and the importance of savings in accordance with the scriptures. The application of stewardship principles with financial literacy training is an opportunity to provide congregants with practical tools for daily living. Although faith-based financial literacy programs are approximately nine percent of all literacy programs they have a considerable rate of success.[122]

Faith-based financial literacy programs are designed to address the unique needs of the congregant. Vitt et. al., (2000) indicated, "Faith-based program managers attributed the success of their intervention to the transformational aspect of the training."[123] Unlike other financial literacy programs, congregants are an integral part of the faith-based entity and have established relationships with the trainers. Frequently, these relationships have been developed over long periods of time and ultimately

---

[120] Dana Jecewiz. *Building Community Through Communicaiton: A Look A UHM's Financial Literacy Program* (New York Univeristy, 2013).
[121] Ibid.
[122] Ibid.
[123] Ibid.

become a powerful resource in the transformation of the congregant. In the faith-based context, confidential information can be shared regarding personal financial challenges and allows the congregant to be candid while obtaining financial guidance and support. Vitt et al., (2000) emphasized, "Reinforcing learning and change, and lifelong attitudes focus on a participant's sense of their spirituality [that] must be engaged. Changes in attitude with regard to debt management are faith-based and that's where training is deemed most successful."[124]

Faith-based financial literacy programs can also provide teaching though sermons and other faith-based activities to support life-long learning objectives. Vitt (2000) et al., reported, "The pastors of these churches stated that finance (and debt) was the 'Last Area of Bondage' for African Americans."[125] Faith-based literacy programs bring to the forefront the origin of their beliefs in alignment with the scriptures. Long held beliefs can be addressed and bring clarity to false notions. According to Vitt (2000), "Another program director explained the church's involvement as a necessary part of its overall teaching: "Unless you have a healthy relationship with money and put things into perspective, you cannot have a good relationship with God."[126] The goal of faith-based financial literacy programs is to integrate spiritual and financial stewardship principles to provide useful strategies for living. Applying financial literacy principles augments important life skills necessary for making informed personal financial decisions.

Faith-based financial literacy curriculum began decades ago with Larry Burkett (1975) who developed tools and curriculum that was comprised of videos, audiocassette tapes, textbooks and workbooks. "These resources can be utilized in a bible study, self study, or other formats suitable for both individuals and groups."[127] Designed as a biblically based curriculum - the information continues to be relevant today. Larry Burkett's offers comprehensive tools with a special focus on personal finances, debt management, short and long-range planning, tithing, investments, and

---

[124] Ibid.
[125] Ibid.
[126] Ibid.
[127] Larry Burkett, *How to Manage Your Money: An In-Depth Bible Study on Personal Finances* (Christian Financial Concepts Inc., Moody Publishers, 1975).

leaving an inheritance to heirs. As a practical study guide, the scriptures are utilized to place biblical principles into a context that imparts specific knowledge and understanding to believers. A crucial element of the faith-based financial literacy-training program is the importance of prayer to focus on an individual's attitude on goal setting, and guidance from the Holy Spirit to empower the believer to remain focused throughout the challenges of life.

CHAPTER THREE

Theological Foundation

God

In Genesis 4:2-5 described the offerings presented to God by Cain and Abel. Abel gave the more excellent sacrifice, which was honored by God. Cain failed to offer his first fruits unto God and as a result God did not honor his gift. God showed Abel favor and Cain became jealous and angry, which led to Abel's death at the hands of his brother Cain.[128] In the book of Moses, God gave a command to establish tithes to support the financial needs of the church, the poor, and the clergy.[129] "God established the tithe in the form of the first fruits to honor Him as an act of obedience and reverence. As a extension of the first two Ten Commandments "I am the Lord your God" and "Thou shall have no other Gods before me." Early in the Old Testament, tithes were offered unto God. Genesis 14:18-20 states, And Melchizedek king of Salem brought forth bread and wine: and he was the priest of the most high God. And he blessed him, and said, Blessed be Abram of the most high God, possessor of heaven and earth: And blessed be the most high God, which hath delivered thine enemies into thy hand. And he gave him tithes of all. [130] Malachi 3:10, tithes are brought into the storehouse in

---

[128] Genesis 4:2-5
[129] Deuteronomy 14:22-23
[130] Genesis 14:18-20

obedience to God's word.[131] Tithes are meant to be the first and best gift given unto God by the people of God for His honor and glory. The expectation then and now - is for all people to bring their sacrifices to God as each one is able to do so. Most important, the tithe is the first fruit given to God and the giver(s) must never set aside the best portions for him or herself.

In the book of Hosea 4:6 the scripture states, "My people are destroyed for lack of knowledge."[132] The word of God offers guidance and direction in the areas of tithing and stewardship practices as a lifestyle which honors saving and investing in contrast to accumulating debt that often fosters both financial and spiritual bondage.

Jesus

Jesus utilized parables to teach the masses and shared His heavenly message to focus on everyday situations. Matthew 7:7 says, "Ask, and it shall be given you; seek, and ye shall find; knock, and it shall be opened to you."[133] Believers are expected to make their requests known to the heavenly Father, seek and find - while in prayer until their requests are granted. Matthew 13:23 says, "But the one who received the seed that fell on good soil is the man who hears the word, understands and then acts accordingly. Then he produces a crop, yielding a hundred, sixty, or thirty times what was sown."[134] Individuals who hear the word of God, understand it, and act upon it will be blessed and become fruitful over and above their original (physical and spiritual) status.

Jesus directs our paths and we reap the benefits by following His course that will lead us to prosperity. II Corinthians 9:7 states, "Each man should give what he has decided in his heart to give, not reluctantly or under compulsion, for God loves a cheerful giver."[135] The heart of the giver symbolizes the intent and is an act of worship.

---

[131] Malachi 3:10
[132] Hosea 4:6
[133] Matthew 7:7
[134] Matthew 13:23
[135] 2 Corinthians 9:7

Rev. Dr. Donna Taylor

Church

Acts 4:34-35 describes the early church as a cohesive body of believers that sacrificed for one another and shared their possessions to benefit the church body as a whole. "There were no needy persons among them. For from time to time those who owned land or houses sold them, brought the money from the sales and put it at the Apostles feet, and it was distributed to anyone as he had need."[136] Believers brought their tithes to the storehouse to support the needs of the church and its mission to serve others. Believers with large resources and land sold what they had and shared the proceeds among those in need. The early church relied exclusively upon tithing to support the faithful body of believers. This is especially noteworthy since the early church suffered greatly under persecution. The body of believers - the church - met in various houses to avoid detection. Tithes and offerings in the form of proceeds from the land sales financially sustained the church body as the gospel was spread far and wide.

Repayment of Debts and Savings for the Future

Romans 13:7 "Render therefore to all their due: if you owe taxes, repay taxes; if revenue, then revenue; if respect then respect; if honor, then honor. It is just and honorable to repay a debt owed to others. Romans 13:8 tells us, "Let no debt remain outstanding, except the debt to love one another, for he who loves his fellowman hath fulfilled the law."[137] The only thing one should owe another is love for their fellowman. The goal of the believer is to love others and this must always be the highest priority – to demonstrate the love of God to all. Believers will be known by the love they show - one to another. Ecclesiastes 5:5 "It is better that thou should not vow than one should vow and not pay." It is more suitable to avoid making a promise than making a promise that cannot be kept. Proverbs 13:11b "He that gathers money little by little makes it grow." Saving regularly over time will build a nest egg for faithful believers who can assist others in need.

---

[136] Act 4:34-35
[137] Romans 13:8

CHAPTER FOUR

Methodology

Research Problem

The financial empowerment intervention at FABCF was designed to examine the knowledge of congregants to adopt Christian stewardship and debt management principles. The goal of the project was to offer basic financial education and skills training as a means to measure knowledge and to offer an opportunity for congregants' to realize their personal financial goals. Individuals expressed concerns with consumer debt and made claims that personal debt posed barriers in their desire to tithe. Congregants also described being overwhelmed with debt and living from paycheck to paycheck. Vitt (2009) found, "There can be cultural and social influences that suggest seeking financial guidance may be frowned upon socially and individuals may not want to seek help."[138] (Appendix F) However, this was not the case during this intervention as congregants volunteered to participate in the intervention.

The learner listened closely to the concerns of the congregants and began to explore the root cause of consumer indebtedness, which congregants claimed to be a major barrier to tithing. This project was not designed to increase tithing among congregants per se, however, it was designed to reduce personal consumer debt and to build savings by applying biblical

---

[138] Lois Vitt et al., *Values-Centered Financial Education Understanding Cultural Influences on Learners' Financial Behaviors* (The Institute for Socio-Financial Studies and the National Endowment for Financial Education NEFE, 2009).

principles to promote financial literacy among congregants. If the financial skills training, allowed congregants to eliminate debt and to increase giving – this would be a win – win for all involved.

Survey Design

The project was based on a quantitative research design with congregants that self-selected to participate in the intervention based upon recruitment through a strategic marketing plan. A pre/post survey instrument was used and is considered the best method available to the social researcher for the learner's context.[139] The survey was comprised of a 5-point Likert scale, which consisted of twenty questions ranging from demographic information to personal financial habits and practices. (Appendix G) First, to avoid bias, the author referred to Fink (How to Ask Survey Questions) to design the survey.[140] Second, the contextual associate linked questions to the hypothesis, goals and objectives. Third, the contextual associate vetted the questions. The topics in the survey included personal credit card use, bill payment history and frequency of credit use in comparison to the use of cash or debit cards. The other topics included the congregants' regular use of a budget, a debt management plan, and whether they had and utilized a checking and/or savings account. Lastly, the congregants were asked if they had a history of indebtedness leading to bankruptcy proceedings or judgments in the court.

During the first session, the survey instrument was administered to each congregant and adequate time was permitted for each person to complete the survey. The pre-survey was administered to seventeen congregants at the beginning of the first session and the post survey was administered at the end of the sixth session to a total of fourteen congregants. Based on the consistent participation of ten (out of twenty) congregants' data was analyzed on ten congregants that completed the pre/post survey. Congregants were asked to include their gender and birthdates for tracking purposes only. An identification number was assigned to each

---

[139] Earl Babbie, *The Basics of Social Research*, Chapman University (Thomson and Wadsworth, 4th Edition, 2008).
[140] Arlene Fink, *How to Ask Survey Questions* (Sage Publishers, 2nd Edition, 2003).

congregant to allow the author to accurately collect the pre/post survey responses and to eliminate bias.

Data Analysis

The Wilcoxon signed-rank test is a nonparametric test, which was selected as it offers the most flexibility in performing data analysis on small (20 combined pre/post test) samples. To analyze the data using the Wilcoxon signed-rank test, a preliminary process was conducted to ensure three assumptions were met first.[141] When the data meets the following three assumptions required for the Wilcoxon signed-rank test the results are considered valid and reliable.[142] The first two assumptions relate to the study design and the types of variables that are measured. The third assumption reflects the nature of the data and is the one assumption tested using SPSS Statistics.[143] The first assumption pertained to the dependent variable that should be measured on an ordinal or continuous level. The ordinal values are placed in a ranking order from smaller to larger. In this case, the 5-point Likert scale was used in the survey instrument. The second assumption is that the dependent variable should consist of two categorical, related groups, or matched pairs. The third assumption is based on comparisons of a pre and a post treatment of the matched pairs.[144]

The Wilcoxon signed-rank test was performed using SPSS to analyze the pre and post survey data. The pre-survey scores of each congregant were added separately and compared to the total scores of the same congregant in the post-survey. The 'p' value is (.045) and is statistically significant, the p-value is the probability of obtaining a test statistic result that rejects the null hypothesis. The confidence interval of 95% is based on the 'p' value of (.045).[145] The 'z' score of 2.00 means the standard deviation is in an acceptable range to reject the null hypothesis.

Survey Results

---

[141] Myles Hollander, Douglas A. Wolfe and Eric Chicken, *Nonparametric Statistical Methods* (John Wiley and Sons, Inc. 2014).
[142] Ibid.
[143] Ibid.
[144] Ibid.
[145] Ibid.

The Wilcoxon signed-rank test compared the congregants' pre/post survey results as it pertained to the knowledge regarding stewardship and debt management principles. The data results indicated a 'z' value 2.00, $p <$ .05 with a confidence interval (CI) of ninety-five percent.[146] The Wilcoxon test measured two samples at two intervals, the pre-treatment and post treatment, which compared a change in the congregants pertaining to their financial literacy knowledge. The independent variables are the stewardship and debt management principles, which remains constant and the dependent variables are the congregants' regarding financial literacy knowledge. (Appendix H)

The Wilcoxon signed-rank test determined the reliability and validity of the data [the reliability, which is the degree to which an assessment tool produces stable and consistent results and validity, which is how well a test measures what it is purported to measure]. [147] The financial literacy empowerment project demonstrated action research as it included "members of a community seeking to improve their financial situation."[148] The learner posits that adults can benefit from acquiring financial literacy skills to manage personal finances, which will ultimately contribute to the financial stability of the church.[149] Stewardship and debt management are key components to measuring the congregants' knowledge regarding the importance of financial literacy. A history of making uninformed financial decisions may be a contributing factor for personal consumer indebtedness.[150]

---

[146] Samuel B. Green and Neil J. Salkind. *Using SPSS for Windows and Macintosh Analyzing and Understanding Data* (Prentice and Hall, Sixth Edition, 2011).

[147] Ibid.

[148] Davydd J. Greenwood and Morten Levin, *Introduction to Action Research: Social Research for Social Change* (Sage Publishers, 1998), 4.

[149] Michael A. Schwartz, *Martin Luther King's Atlanta Church Adds Financial Literacy Training*, 2010, USATODAY http://usatoday30.usatoday.com/news/religion/2010-04-09-kingchurch8_ST_N.htm accessed on September 20, 2012.

[150] Annamaria Lusardi, The *Importance of Financial Literacy* (National Bureau of Economic Research, NBER Reporter: Research Summary 2009). www.nber.org/reporter/2009number2/lusardi.htm assessed online on September 12, 2012.

The Hypothesis Statement

Hypothesis: If the selected members of the FABCF congregation are exposed to stewardship principles by direct instruction, then there will be an increase of knowledge among membership to establish a Financial Empowerment Ministry. Null Hypothesis: If the selected members of the FABCF congregation are exposed to stewardship principles by direct instruction, then there will not be an increase of knowledge among membership to establish a Financial Empowerment Ministry.

Discussion

Ten congregants completed the pre-survey in week one and the post-survey in week six (20 total for the pre/post survey results). The hypothesis was accepted based on the 95% confidence interval and a *'p'* value of < .05 (.045 actual). The response to the financial literacy training underscored the impact of the congregants' knowledge based on the instruction and sharing of information among other congregants[151] There were four themes that emerged from the survey questionnaire, which measured the congregants' financial knowledge and practices. The first theme focused on the congregants' use of a household budget to manage their personal finances. In the pre survey six of the ten respondents stated that they used a budget to manage finances. In the post survey nine out of ten responded they would use a budget to better manage their personal finances. Only one respondent stated they were undecided whether they would use a budget to manage their finances. In the pre survey, fifty percent stated that they paid their bills by the due date each month and fifty percent stated they often paid late fees for overdue bills. In the post survey, only one of the ten responded they were not likely to pay their bills on time in the future.

The second theme involved congregants' management of consumer credit to achieve personal goals. In the pre survey, seven out of ten congregants' responded to the question that managing debt was a high priority in their lives. In the post survey all ten congregants said managing debt was a high priority. In the pre survey, fifty percent stated they did

---

[151] Nancy T. Ammerman et al., *Studying Congregations: A New Handbook* (Abingdon Press Nashville, 1998),111.

not seek God's guidance in managing personal debt. In the post survey all respondents stated they would begin to seek God's guidance to resolve issues pertaining to debt management. In the pre survey, three of ten considered using bankruptcy as a remedy for resolving debt. In the post survey, only one of the respondents stated they would still consider bankruptcy as a viable option to resolve debt. In addition, all respondents stated they used cash to pay for purchases and did not rely exclusively on credit card transactions or payday loans. Three of the ten respondents stated they had outstanding credit card debt ranging from between three hundred to twelve thousand dollars.

The third theme was associated with having a savings account in the event of an emergency. In the pre survey, five respondents stated they had a savings account in the event of an emergency and five stated they did not. In the post survey, eight recognized the importance of a savings account, one disagreed and one respondent was neutral. In the pre survey, four out of ten respondents stated they borrowed from friends and relatives and that friends and relatives also borrowed from them. In the post survey, six of the ten respondents stated they would not allow friends and relatives borrow money from them and they did would not lend money to others.

The fourth theme captured the congregants' general knowledge about money and financial habits or practices. All respondents stated they had a checking account and four stated they experienced overdraft fees from time to time. All respondents stated money management was important to them and they wanted to learn more about managing their finances. In the pre survey, six out of ten did not know where to access information to improve their money management skills. In the post survey, nine out of ten knew where to access information to improve their personal money management skills.

The responses to the post survey highlighted how diligent the congregants' became about managing their finances. Although most of the congregants attended church regularly and were exposed to the stewardship presentations, and sermons only fifty percent relied on God's guidance to resolve debt. Furthermore, congregants' were less likely to seek assistance from the diaconate ministry. This is quite striking and supports the research that individuals will conform to what their peers are doing around them. If individuals perceive other congregants are not likely to seek help then they too are not likely to seek help in managing their personal finances.[152]

Studies That Have Addressed the Problem

The author identified three studies that addressed a deficiency regarding financial literacy skills in faith-based settings. In 2013, Indiana University School of Philanthropy published the Congregational Economic Impact Study and sampled 3,103 congregations, which was designed to measure knowledge pertaining to finances after the economic recession of 2008.[153] The survey examined congregations across various denominations and faith traditions. An assessment of "Financial education in the form of workshops, classes and seminars were an integral part of church life according to thirty-six percent of respondents. This meant that more than sixty percent of the churches did not offer financial education to their congregants."[154] Similar to the intervention at FABCF, training was offered to large groups and when the church is unable to provide members with financial assistance, financial counseling was offered instead."

Another similarity included teaching stewardship principles over the pulpit or during other ministry activities [such as bible study] that allowed information to be disseminated among the congregants."[155] A significant finding in the study demonstrated distinct differences among congregations. In particular, historically Black Protestant churches were less likely to receive either an endowment or a bequest.[156] Notably, Black Protestant churches frequently do not have a long-term financial endowment or a bequest to rely upon during financially challenging times.

In a 2013 study entitled, "The Influence of Financial Literacy on Faith-Based Epistemology: A Case Study of Arizona Church Members reinforced the awareness of actionable financial knowledge that was

---

[152] Ibid.
[153] Una Osili, *The Economic Congregational Economic Impact Study* (Indiana University School of Philanthropy, 2013), 5.
[154] Ibid.
[155] Ibid.
[156] Ibid.

necessary to increase financial literacy."[157] It was important for program leaders to identify an individual's stage of readiness, which facilitates an individual's inclination to learn financial literacy skills. Blake and Vucetic (2013) found, "There was a gap between faith-based epistemology and the influence of financial literacy based on cognitive behaviors."[158] The intervention at FABCF, did not require a readiness assessment prior to exposing individuals to financial literacy skills – in discussions with congregants - it was apparent there was a need. It is important to note, assessment of an individual's readiness to change, prior to beginning the intervention, can be cost prohibitive and time intensive for faith-based programs. It is noteworthy, that the inter-personal relationships established between the clergy and congregants often reveals the need for financial literacy training based upon various personal interactions.

In the 2013 study entitled "Starving Payday Lenders: Targeted Faith-Centered Financial Literacy Training in a Context of Concentrated Poverty identified hidden symptoms of financial illiteracy." The use of Payday lenders and other non-banking services are key indicators of an individual's poverty level. The reliance on non-banking services was also substantiated by the lack of choices available to individuals living in poverty. The ability to acquire a credit report or possess financial resources to qualify for commercial banking services is rarely an option for individuals living in poverty. "Persons living in poverty or experiencing financial hardship are often not recognized by clergy or church leadership."[159] Similarly, at FABCF the church leadership attributed an aversion to tithing to a lack of spiritual maturity or obedience to the Word of God. Frequently, personal financial hardship is attributed to a lack of discipline and a failure to control spending habits, which is only a small element of this pervasive problem. Randy White (2013) found, "Motivated adults benefit from targeted financial literacy education and goals are attained by utilizing an interactive curriculum.[160]

---

[157] Joseph M. Blake Jr. and Jelena Vucetic, *The Influence of Financial Literacy on Faith-Based Epistemology: A Case Study of Arizona Church* Members (International Journal of Social Science Research, 2013), 27.
[158] Ibid.
[159] *Training in a Context of Concentrated Poverty*, http://transformedcentralvalley.org accessed August 1, 2013.
[160] Ibid.

CHAPTER FIVE

Field Experience

The first phase of the field experience included financial literacy education and training through classroom instruction and webinars. (Appendix J) Classroom instruction was obtained through George Washington School of Business in Washington, D.C. The Financial Literacy Seminar Series (FLSS) is a joint initiative between the Board of Governors of the Federal Reserve System and the George Washington School of Business. The FLSS is offered biannually and was comprised of six or more presentations by world-renowned economists and researchers. The financial literacy discussions explored how African Americans, students, military personnel, senior citizens/retirees, low and moderate-income families, and educators manage financial decisions. Dr. Annamaria Lusardi noted,

> Every segment of society is affected by financial literacy and research is designed to identify financial literacy tools and methods to improve financial capability. The FLSS forum's research findings are shared among researchers to provide an opportunity for further collaboration and to develop models for future research. The esteemed faculty members of the FLSS Forum included, Dr. Annamaria Lusardi, Denit Trust Distinguished Scholar in Economics and Accountancy has contributed immensely to financial literacy research over the years. Dr. Lusardi and her colleagues have published numerous research articles pertaining to financial literacy. Prior to her tenure as

faculty and chair of the Global Financial Literacy Excellence Center at George Washington University, Dr. Lusardi previously held a faculty position at Dartmouth for over twenty years. Dr. Lusardi and her colleagues have worked on several projects regarding financial education in both the United States and abroad. She has advised the Dartmouth Hitchcock medical center, FINRA investor education foundation, the Dutch Central bank, the OECD, and the World Bank on issues related to financial literacy and saving. In 2009, she served as a faculty advisor for the office of financial education of the United States Treasury. Dr. Lusardi was recently recognized by the New York Times as one of the six most influential economists in the area of financial reform. Prof. Lusardi is also a member of the steering committee of the FLSS. (George Washington School of Business, Financial Literacy Seminar Series) [161]

The author's field experience also included the financial empowerment intervention that was comprised of six sessions held at First Agape Baptist Community of Faith in January through February of 2014. The celebration event was held in the church sanctuary during the 11:00 a.m. worship service on Sunday, February 23rd. The Financial Empowerment intervention's marketing and promotion campaign utilized resources such as the church bulletin, emails, text messaging, postcards, phone calls, church school and morning worship service announcements, the worship service prayer circle and personal contact. (Appendices K – O)

The intervention was developed as a model to improve financial literacy skills based on congregants' interest in addressing financial barriers to tithing due and consumer indebtedness. Brooke Stephens (1997) wrote, "The most difficult first step is to review the knowledge that has kept us from developing a money focused mentality and to see ourselves as

---

[161] George Washington School of Business, *Financial Literacy Seminar Series (FLSS)* http://business.gwu.edu/faculty/annamaria_lusardi.cfm accessed on June 15, 2014.

financial beings."[162] The financial empowerment intervention was designed to measure a change in knowledge regarding the use of stewardship and debt management principles among congregants at FABCF. The planning phase began with the marketing and promotion campaign to increase awareness regarding the intervention, which included a chance for an individual to win one hundred dollars during the first, second and final sessions.

On the initial day of the intervention, the author provided an overview of the goals and objectives for the congregants to obtain. The pre-survey was completed by seventeen congregants and designed to measure their baseline financial literacy knowledge and habits. The pre-survey also provided insight into their level of knowledge pertaining to personal financial decision-making skills. The pre-survey was also an opportunity to collect demographic information such as gender, age, and the congregants' current level of consumer debt pertaining to credit cards, Payday loans, and student loans. Personal financial decisions are often a reflection of financial literacy knowledge and its application as it applies to debt prevention and management, and saving for emergencies.

The first session included an overview of stewardship principles with scriptural references and learning the basics of budgeting. The two facilitators were (led by FABCF Deacon Ministry) which, provided detailed instructions on the principles of budgeting, and individualized budget plans designed to meet the unique needs of the congregants. The congregants had an opportunity to ask the facilitators questions pertaining to their individual financial circumstances.

Session One - Saturday, January 18, 2014 – 10:00 a.m. – 12 noon

God's Blueprint for Personal Finance & Creating a Budget

The author read the 24th Psalm, opened the session in prayer, and introduced the topic of financial literacy and the importance of acquiring financial skills to enhance stewardship responsibilities in the church. The congregants included ministry leaders such as the church treasurer,

---

[162] Brooke Stephens, *Talking Dollars and Making Sense – A Wealth Building Guide For African-Americans* (McGraw-Hill Publishers,1997).

ministry chairpersons, trustees, and members of the church budget and finance ministry. To jumpstart the first session, three congregants received door prizes, which could be used to support their personal financial tasks and responsibilities. The learning objectives were: 1) To discuss key scriptures illustrating God's wealth; 2) To explain God's design for managing financial blessings and 3) To apply biblical principles in our financial decisions.

The Pastor, Rev. Dr. Daniel L. Brown, was present and is one of two adjunct faculty for this research project. Dr. Brown commented on the importance of this project for the life of the church and its benefit to First Agape Baptist Community of Faith (FABCF). In essence, the first session introduced scriptures pertaining to financial stewardship. In addition, the congregants learned how to create a budget and to include the tithe as the first budget entry followed by their other household expenses. The final drawing of the day was a chance to win $100. The awardee was selected and vowed to bring her tithe to the storehouse on Sunday.

Deacon Taylor, the lead facilitator announced there would be a chance to win $50 during the second session and a chance to win $100 during the final session. Five of the congregants stated that they would be unable to attend session two due to prior ministry commitments and personal obligations. There were seventeen congregants present at the first session. (Appendix P)

Session Two - Saturday, January 25, 2014 – 10:00 – 11:30 a.m.

Godly Tools for Debt Prevention

The author read the 15th Psalm, opened the session in prayer, introduced the topic of debt and the pitfalls of debt, and awarded three door prizes. There were nine congregants present at the second session. The group activities were then turned over to the facilitators (Deacon Taylor and Deacon McKoy). The learning objectives were: 1) To discuss key scriptures to illustrate the pitfalls of debt; 2) To create a budget to prevent debt using God's order for finances; and 3) To create a plan to eliminate debt and to restore a positive credit rating.

The first activity involved evaluating a budget for a single male aged twenty years old, living alone earning $1,331 per month. The congregants were placed in two groups to discuss whether the individual had the ability to repay a $2K loan for a career-training program with the future potential of earning 90K annually. The activity involved finding a strategy to streamline the subject's monthly expenses to accommodate a loan repayment plan. Based on the first workshop the congregants used a rubric that they were given to follow God's order for finances to avoid the pitfalls of debt. The congregants made recommendations to establish whether the single adult male was moving toward debt or away from debt.

The second activity based on information gathered in this first assessment, determined whether the single male in the case study, was moving towards or away from the pitfalls of debt. The recommendations were based on God's blueprint for finance and following God's order of finance. After each activity there was a scripture reference and reinforcement of the pitfalls of debt and God's financial freedom when one follows God's plan.

In the final activity, the congregants were asked to submit anonymous questions on a sheet of paper regarding personal examples of their credit card debt and credit scores. The question pertaining to credit cards would be explored during the third financial workshop. The questions submitted by the congregants were particularly meaningful, as they addressed personal scenarios that would be discussed within the groups. The drawing for fifty dollars was awarded and the author closed the session in prayer. (Appendix Q)

Session Three - Saturday, February 1, 2014 - 10:00 – 11:30 a.m.

Godly Tools for Debt Management

The third session opened by reading the 1st Psalm and prayer by the author. Several congregants' names were randomly selected to receive door prizes that would support their ability to maintain accurate financial records. The goal was to prepare congregants to manage consumer debt. The learning objectives were: 1) To discuss principles of financial literacy to reduce consumer debt; 2) To explain strategies to eliminate specific types of consumer debt; and 3) To create a short and long term debt management plan. The focus of the session was to create separate debt repayment plans for credit cards, payday loans, and mortgage loans. Door prizes were distributed by a random selection of names at the beginning of the session. Fourteen congregants were placed in three workgroups and were asked to examine a scenario involving a newlywed couple that wanted to borrow $1,230 to purchase furniture for their new apartment. The congregants were asked to calculate the interest rate and to compare repayment plans at three different interest rates. At the end of the session, Deacon Taylor provided a summary of the lesson and one person was randomly selected to win $50. The author asked the congregants [as a preventive measure] to consider planning ahead to decide - in advance - how to spend their tax refund as many expected to receive one in the next few months. The congregants were encouraged to pray prior to receiving a tax refund and to carefully decide how to repay debt and to begin saving for emergencies. Most important, if congregants were considering a tax refund loan, it was important to know the fees they would incur were likely to be cost prohibitive. The author thanked everyone and ended the session in prayer. (Appendix R)

Session Four - Saturday, February 8, 2014 - 10:00 – 11:30 a.m.

The Five W's of Emergency Savings

The author opened in prayer and introduced the session by reading Ecclesiastes 3:1-8. The focus was to learn strategies that would encourage initiating an emergency savings account. The learning objectives were: 1) To discuss biblical principles on the importance of financial savings; 2) To create an emergency savings plan; and 3) To activate an emergency savings fund. The facilitators creatively began the first interactive session by asking these questions: 1) Why should you initiate an emergency savings account? 2) When should you initiate an emergency savings account? 3) Where should you initiate an emergency savings account? 4) Who should initiate an emergency savings account? a) Students preparing for college b) Parents w/children in college and c) Young adults or retirees d) What is the purpose of an emergency savings account? e) To go on vacation; f) Shop for Christmas g) Extra money when your funds are low h) none of the above.

5) Where should you place an emergency savings account? a) Under the mattress is the safest place b) Savings account c) In a checking account.

6) When should an individual initiate an emergency savings account? a) When they receive a bonus or tax refund b) During a financial emergency c) Never- since they can borrow from a family member. 7) Why should you initiate an emergency savings account? a) To avoid high interest payday loans b) To spend during Christmas time and c) None of the above (Appendix S).

Session Five - Saturday, February 15, 2014 - 10:00 – 11:30 a.m.

Creating a Financial and Spiritual Legacy

The session was opened by introducing the topic of a financial and spiritual legacy in the lives of believers. 1 Kings 2:1-4 was read and the author initiated the prayer. The facilitators, Deacon Taylor and Deacon McKoy described purpose of Estate Planning and how to use stewardship to formalize a spiritual and financial legacy. The learning objectives were: At the completion of the workshop, students will be able to: a) To discuss biblical principles on the importance of estate planning b) To discuss the essential components of an estate plan and c) To initiate a family dialogue and legacy activities for an estate plan. The legacy plan involves discussions with family members pertaining to the distribution of possessions, selection of an executor, and sharing thoughts regarding faith and values. A discussion regarding a family legacy also included documenting (in written form) the caregiving needs of dependent family members, future educational pursuits, dissolution of property, and end of life decisions and requests. The congregants described utilizing opportunities such as family gatherings, reunions, and meetings to share specific desires and plans with loved ones. The ultimate goal was to establish a last 'Will and Testament' that would be revised and updated as needed and to inform key persons of the contents. The congregants were encouraged to discuss the contents of their Will with legal counsel and tax experts to ensure the elements follow the Virginia State guidelines, and as a legal and binding document. The congregants first worked individually and then participated in groups to address the following topics: 1) What is an estate plan? 2) Why should an estate plan be created? 3) When should an estate plan be created? 4) How do you create an estate plan? 5) Who will receive my financial and personal assets? 6) Who will manage my legal and personal affairs? 7) Who will be responsible for my dependents upon my death? 8) What are my wishes for a Home Going Celebration (burial or cremation)? The session ended by summarizing the importance of estate planning and to discuss with family members within twenty-four to forty-eight hours of the workshop. At the conclusion of the session, one cash door prize was awarded and the congregants were reminded that there would be a final session. The author ended the session in prayer. (Appendix T)

Session Six - Saturday, February 22, 2014 - 10:00 a.m. – 12 noon

Applying Stewardship and Debt Management

The author began the last session by reading the 67th Psalm and opened in prayer. There were thirteen congregants present of which only ten were eligible to complete the post-survey that would be administered at the conclusion of the session. The learning objectives were: 1) Summarize biblical principles on debt management and financial stewardship. 2) Apply Christian decision-making skills to reduce consumer debt. 3) Create short and long term financial goals. Deacon McKoy summarized the financial empowerment workshop goals and objectives. The facilitators initiated a group discussion by asking the congregants to write their personal views on a piece of paper and to describe what they learned during the first five sessions. The facilitators read each reflection aloud and one congregant was randomly selected to win a cash award of $20. The congregants were placed in three groups and asked to a plan short, intermediate, and a long-range goal for a single twenty-four year old with an annual gross income of 24K living with parents and a desire to rent an apartment. The short-term goal would be to payoff his car loan at $240 per month. The intermediate goal would be to pay off his student loan at a rate of $700 per month. The long-range goal is to continue to live with his parents and to save money until he had accumulated one month's rent and one month's security deposit of 2K. At the conclusion of the session, the congregants completed the post-survey and a name was randomly selected to win $100 in cash. The congregants were reminded of the award ceremony that would take place during the next day during Sunday morning worship service. The author prayed over the luncheon that was provided and the session ended shortly thereafter. (Appendix U)

Session Seven – Worship Service - Sunday, February 23, 2014 - 10:00 – 11:30 a.m.

The Celebration

The celebration was conducted for the congregants that participated in the six-week intervention that culminated the following day during Sunday morning worship service. The author provided a brief overview of the project intervention to the congregation regarding the importance of financial literacy training skills, debt prevention and management and establishing a savings account. There were twenty-three certificates presented to the congregants. Ten congregants received a certificate of completion for attending every session of the intervention. Ten congregants received a certificate of participation for attending fewer than six sessions. [Congregants were encouraged to participate as time their permitted]. A total of twenty-one congregants attended at least one session, which allowed them exposure to financial literacy information, although limited in nature]. Rev. Dr. Daniel L. Brown received a certificate for leadership, and for his role as adjunct faculty member. The facilitators, Deacon David L. Taylor and Deacon Herb McKoy received a certificate for their stellar work as facilitators during the six-week intervention. The congregants that were not present received their certificates at a later date.

CHAPTER SIX

Summary

Several congregants expressed their appreciation for the training they received and had a desire to participate in training in the future. The three congregants sought individual financial counseling to rectify matters of indebtedness and to build assets such as savings accounts to weather emergencies. The congregants demonstrated an interest in establishing their Last Will and Testament and planned to consult with a legal professional. Congregants also planned to discuss pertinent details with family members to make their personal end-of-life wishes known.

Financial literacy training is an opportunity to educate and to inform congregants who are most vulnerable to financial shocks. Individuals that are equipped with financial literacy skills are more capable of making informed financial decisions. Financial literacy training that is interactive and replicates real world experiences can facilitate the adoption of these newly acquired skills. Financial empowerment training can also be used to promote the use of stewardship and debt management principles to improve financial decisions. The church is responsible for empowering congregants and to promote spiritual, social, and financial growth opportunities to aid in the maturation of the believer. The Black church plays a vital role in the life of African Americans and to teach congregants about the importance of learning financial literacy skills to positively impact every facet of their lives.

CONCLUSION

Seeking strategies to prevent, manage debt, and save for emergencies will become a necessity for the economic survival of African American congregants now and in the future. Living with significant levels of consumer debt is clearly unsustainable. For many, stagnant wages, unemployment and underemployment will influence the ability to learn and practice financial literacy skills. To actively address the financial needs of African Americans, the church is solely responsible for the wholistic development of its congregants. The church must employ practical strategies to improve the prevalence of low financial literacy among congregants. It is significant to note that African Americans' purchasing power has a potential to be a powerful economic force that can impact the church and the African American community in substantive ways if used strategically. If the church fails to seize the moment to empower its congregants' to effectively use their economic resources in the African American community, other entities with less altruistic objectives will fill this void.

Self-help and interdependence is paramount to begin building financial skills and knowledge among African American youth and young adults. Economic self-determination is closely linked with the political and social freedoms Americans enjoy in a capitalistic society. Furthermore, to thrive in a capitalistic society, African Americans must become more financially savvy and employ methods to reduce the level of economic marginalization and predatory business practices that currently exist in the United States.

These research findings have launched two financial literacy initiatives that have future implications for the community-at-large. First, the author's secular vocation at the Department of Veterans Affairs has found military Veterans also experience challenges with financial literacy. There are studies that support the rise in homelessness among Veterans may be linked to low financial literacy. In 2014, the Veterans Health Administration leadership within the Department of Veterans Affairs, agreed to allow the author to add knowledge of financial literacy to the public health grant program criteria. Through the annual public health grant program Veterans will receive financial literacy training.

Second, Rev. Brown will launch the Agape Bible Institute in January 2015 and the author will teach courses on Christian Stewardship and Debt Management Principles.

REFLECTIONS

Recommendations for Future Researchers

Recommendations for future researchers includes the utilization of social media in the form of text messaging and/or email messages to cue congregants to build and fortify their emergency savings accounts in regular intervals. Although adopting stewardship and debt management principles was a key feature of the financial empowerment intervention, the ultimate goal was to motivate congregants to establish or to enlarge an existing savings account. The use of computer technology in the form of social media can be a valuable communication tool and is currently being utilized by many organizations. Reliance on social media has become a way of life for many Americans and is an opportunity to capitalize on the latest technology and to provide targeted financial literacy messaging. Today, congregants lead extremely busy lives and it is crucial that efforts are made to recognize the most effective methods to assist them in achieving their personal financial goals.

The second recommendation for future researchers would be to examine the benefits of online banking. Today's consumer is challenged with reconciling their bank account balances in a timely manner and can be empowered by utilizing online banking products via computer or smartphone. Training for online banking skills can equip congregants to regularly monitor their personal finances. Monitoring bank accounts by utilizing online banking may also be a remedy to avoid expensive overdraft fees that can be costly to individuals with limited financial resources. Online banking can offer regular and timed payments to creditors using online bill pay. The checkbook or the monthly bank statement is currently considered an outdated modality and financial institutions are moving toward eliminating paper transactions in the near future. Increasingly, consumers are using smartphones or a computer tablets (such as the Ipad), which facilitates the ease of use regarding electronic or online banking. The commercial banking consumer that is unable to utilize web-based banking services will soon be at a disadvantage without access to these latest technologies. It is crucial that individuals remain knowledgeable regarding the electronic products that are available for the banking consumer.

The third recommendation for future researchers is to promote the use of targeted public service announcements and campaigns to increase savings on a broader scale through local, state, and national Baptist conventions. In general, low financial literacy is a national concern and especially within the African American community. The promotion of a wide scale 'savings' campaign can be useful for the individual as well as faith-based organizations. Financial initiatives can stimulate changes through faith-based organizations that are adversely affected by the levels of low financial literacy among congregants. Faith-based organizations may rely exclusively on the financial support of their member churches to operate and must be proactive in educating congregants about the importance of financial literacy skills.

The fourth recommendation for future researchers is to examine the feasibility of establishing a faith-based credit union (on a wide scale) to create a means of supporting African American communities, churches, and educational institutions. Discriminatory banking practices that target African American communities have been financially detrimental. As banks continue to restrict lending in certain sectors of the population, loans for small businesses and groups with unproven financial track records are at an even greater disadvantage. For this reason, African Americans would benefit greatly by supporting the establishment of banking institutions that are sensitive to their financial needs. Credit unions typically provide free financial literacy courses to account holders on topics such as home and auto purchases, saving for college, preparing for retirement, and estate planning. As a banking entity, credit unions are nonprofit money cooperatives whose members can borrow from pooled deposits at lower interest rates.

The fifth and final recommendation for future researchers is to design a pipeline of financial planners, accountants, and financial educators to permeate faith-based organizations within the African American community. Promoting careers in the financial sector among congregants is a means to develop expertise regarding finances and investments within the body of Christ. Furthermore, in partnership with faith-based credit unions, these experts would be encouraged to support African American financial institutions, and provide on-going financial education to churches, and the community-at-large.

As the church considers the financial future of its congregants, it must embrace a new normal and learn to thrive in a capitalistic society and to remember the sacrifices and contributions their ancestors made upon their arrival in the Americas almost four hundred years ago.

EPILOGUE

In the 21st century financial literacy and debt management skills is as important for Americans as academic skills. As clergy and ministry leaders it is incumbent upon us to promote financial education that will edify the body of Christ and our communities at large. To the degree we can provide this necessary skills by training our families, congregations, and communities will be able to face financial setbacks and challenges.

Although financial literacy education is taught in many school and higher institutes of learning it is sporadic at best. Employers and financial institutions such as credit unions frequently offer financial education at no cost. Many credit unions offer financial free financial literacy education to their members and non-members alike and it is a valuable resource to the community. In 2017, student loan debt and inadequate retirement savings may become the next crisis we face in the United States and we must acquire the financial literacy skills to survive and to thrive.

APPENDIX A

Financial Literacy Questions

> **Assessment Designed by Lusardi and Mitchell (2008, 2011)**
>
> 1. Suppose you had $100 in a savings account and the interest rate was 2 percent per year. After 5 years, how much do you think you would have in the account if you left the money to grow: [**more than $102;** exactly $102 less than $102 do not know; refuse to answer.]
> 2. Imagine that the interest rate on your savings account was 1 percent per year and inflations was 2 percent per year. After 1 year, would you be able to buy [more than, exactly the same as or **less than today** with the money in this account; do no know; refuse to answer.]
> 3. Do you think that the following statement is true or false? "Buying a single company stock usually provides a safer return that a stock mutual fund." [true; **false**; do not know; refuse to answer]

APPENDIX B

Financial Wheel

- EARN
  - 30 days
  - Annually

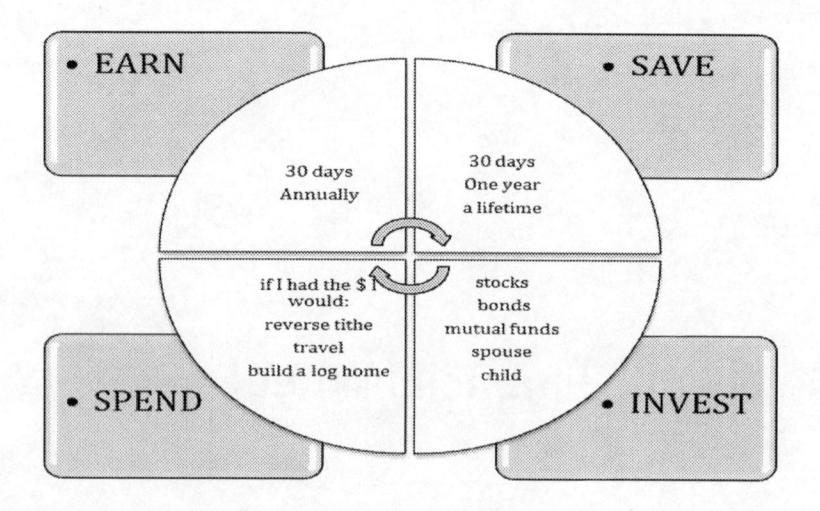

- SAVE
  - 30 days
  - One year
  - a lifetime

- SPEND
  - if I had the $1 would:
  - reverse tithe
  - travel
  - build a log home

- INVEST
  - stocks
  - bonds
  - mutual funds
  - spouse
  - child

Jacquette M Timmons – Financial Behaviorist
www.jacquettetimmons.com/make-money-pleasurable

APPENDIX C

Financial Literacy Education Program Sectors

Rev. Dr. Donna Taylor

Financial Literacy Education Program Sectors

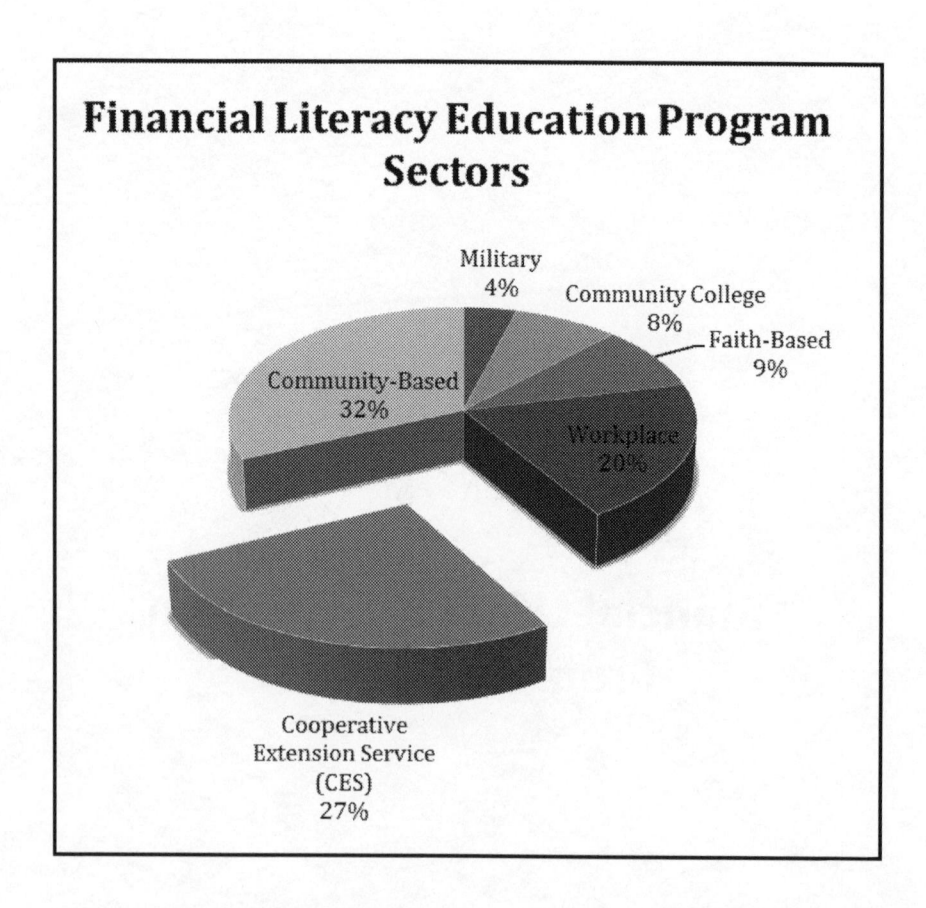

- Military 4%
- Community College 8%
- Faith-Based 9%
- Workplace 20%
- Cooperative Extension Service (CES) 27%
- Community-Based 32%

Figure 1: Flows of Cultural Influence on Consumer Financial Behaviors

Vitt et al., *Personal Finance and the Rush to Competence: Financial Literacy Education in the U.S.*, The Fannie Mae Foundation, and Institute for Socio-Financial Studies, 2001.

APPENDIX D

Maslow's Hierarchy of Needs

Rev. Dr. Donna Taylor

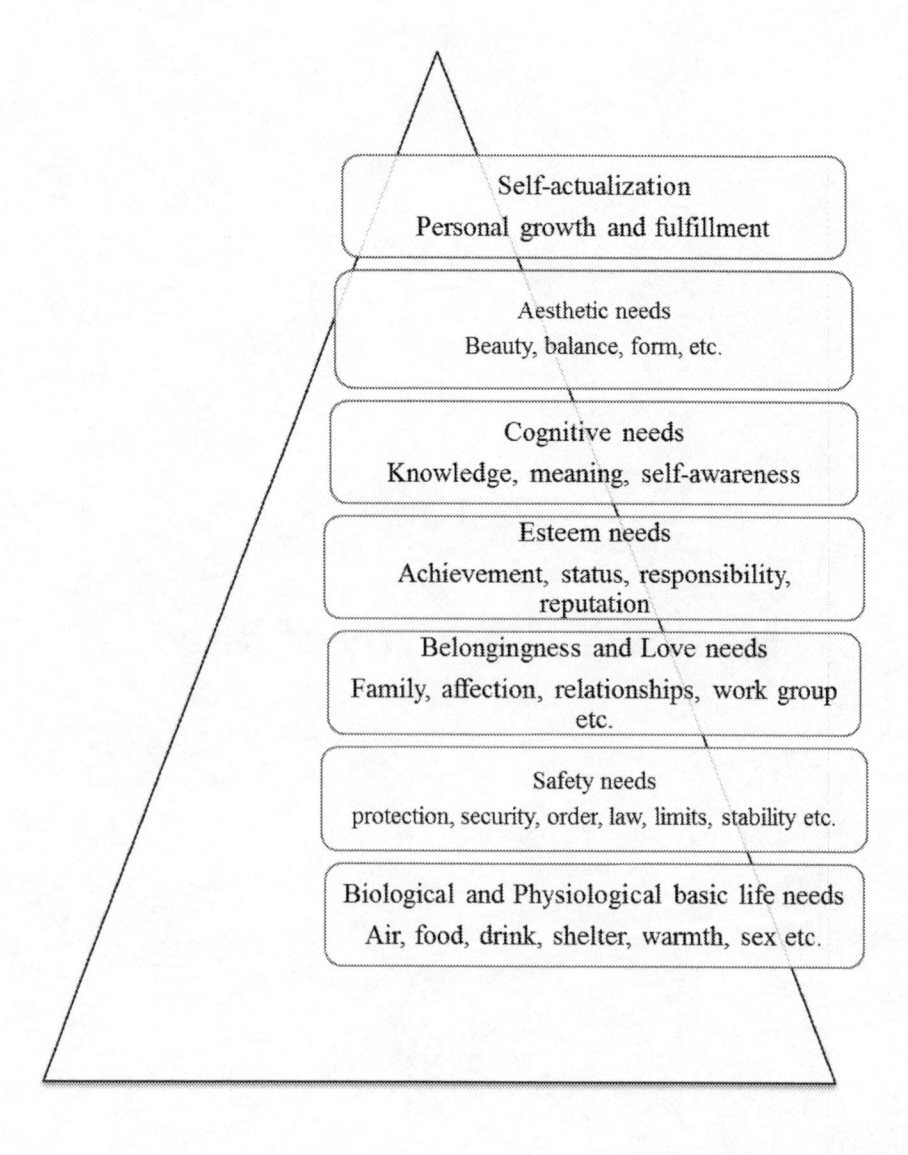

Self-actualization
Personal growth and fulfillment

Aesthetic needs
Beauty, balance, form, etc.

Cognitive needs
Knowledge, meaning, self-awareness

Esteem needs
Achievement, status, responsibility, reputation

Belongingness and Love needs
Family, affection, relationships, work group etc.

Safety needs
protection, security, order, law, limits, stability etc.

Biological and Physiological basic life needs
Air, food, drink, shelter, warmth, sex etc.

APPENDIX E

Maslow's Law Explanation

In 1954, Abraham Maslow published his research and findings on the basis of motivation.
He called it the Hierarchy of Human Needs. This simple idea has become a fundamental framework for understanding how people are motivated and how they become successful and productive. The hierarchy is represented as a tiered triangle, where each tier must be achieved before the next tier can be reached.

The bottom four tiers are called 'deficiency needs'. These are the basic needs the all people need to fulfill and are necessary before an individual can become successful and productive. The top tier is a 'growth need'. A growth need doesn't go away, but serves to motivate one further. Let's examine each tier as it applies to motivation;

Tiers 1 & 2 – Physiological and Safety Needs
Conventionally, employers only took care of physiological needs – the need for food, water, clothing and necessities to support life. They quickly found that only taking care of the most basic of needs wasn't enough to motivate employees. Chances are that individual's feel secure in their physiological needs.

Tiers 3 & 4 – Belonging and Esteem Needs
Before individual's can effectively be creative, ethical, effective problem solvers and otherwise reach the level of self-actualization, they need to have their Belonging and Esteem needs met. This is where most Individuals find challenges with technical professionals and where The Optimal Self focuses. Giving an individual the tools to build their self esteem, gain respect from others and find confidence can be very difficult. While you can directly control the most basic needs (tiers 1 & 2), you can only give employees the tools to fulfilling these, more complicated, needs. Without satisfying belonging and esteem needs, an individual will never do their best.

Tier 5 – Self Actualization
When you take care of an individual's physiological, safety, belonging and esteem needs, they can truly do their best. Self Actualization is the point where an individual shines, creates his best ideas, loves to work, and puts everything he can into his profession. You only find individual's at this level of productivity that motivates them through fulfilling their needs.

Dana Jecewiz. 2013. *Building Community Through Communicaiton: A Look A UHM's Financial*
Literacy Program, New York Univeristy. http://danajecewiz.weebly.com/uploads/1/8/0/0/18001767/d.jecewiz-financial_literacy.pdfAccessed on August 8, 2014.

APPENDIX F

Flows of Social Influence on Consumer Financial Behavior

Rev. Dr. Donna Taylor

Flows of Social Influence on Consumer Financial Behavior

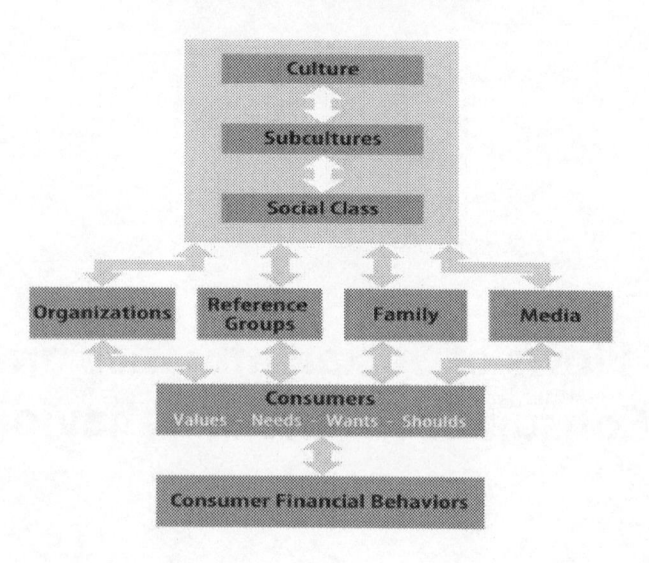

```
              ┌─────────┐
              │ Culture │
              └────┬────┘
                   ↕
            ┌────────────┐
            │ Subcultures│
            └─────┬──────┘
                  ↕
            ┌────────────┐
            │Social Class│
            └────────────┘
   ↙          ↕      ↕       ↘
┌──────────┐ ┌─────────┐ ┌──────┐ ┌─────┐
│Organiza- │ │Reference│ │Family│ │Media│
│tions     │ │ Groups  │ │      │ │     │
└──────────┘ └─────────┘ └──────┘ └─────┘
   ↘          ↕      ↕       ↙
      ┌─────────────────────────────┐
      │         Consumers           │
      │Values - Needs - Wants - Shoulds│
      └──────────────┬──────────────┘
                     ↕
      ┌─────────────────────────────┐
      │ Consumer Financial Behaviors│
      └─────────────────────────────┘
```

Vitt, Lois et al., *Values-Centered Financial Education Understanding Cultural Influences on Learners' Financial Behaviors,* The Institute for Socio-Financial Studies (ISFS) and the National Endowment for Financial Education NEFE, 2009.

APPENDIX G

Stewardship and Debt Management - Pre/Post Survey

M / F circle one Birth Date: Month____Year_____

1. Managing debt is a high priority in my personal finances.
   <u>Strongly agree | Agree | Neutral | Disagree | Strongly disagree</u>
        5   4   3   2   1

2. I seek God's guidance to help me with credit card debt.
   <u>Strongly agree | Agree | Neutral | Disagree | Strongly disagree</u>
        5   4   3   2   1

3. I discuss financial matters with my children and other family members.
   <u>Strongly agree | Agree | Neutral | Disagree | Strongly disagree</u>
        5   4   3   2   1

4. I use cash for most of my purchases.
   <u>Strongly agree | Agree | Neutral | Disagree | Strongly disagree</u>
        5   4   3   2   1

5. I would like to learn how to manage my money better.
   <u>Strongly agree | Agree | Neutral | Disagree | Strongly disagree</u>
        5   4   3   2   1

6. I am in debt and have considered filing bankruptcy.
   <u>Strongly agree | Agree | Neutral | Disagree | Strongly disagree</u>
        5   4   3   2   1

7. I pay my bills by the due date every month.
   <u>Strongly agree | Agree | Neutral | Disagree | Strongly disagree</u>
        5   4   3   2   1

8. I often pay late fees for overdue bills.
   <u>Strongly agree | Agree | Neutral | Disagree | Strongly disagree</u>
        5   4   3   2   1

9. I know where to access information on managing my money better.
   Strongly agree | Agree | Neutral | Disagree | Strongly disagree
   5   4   3   2   1

10. I use a budget to manage my income and to pay my bills.
    Strongly agree | Agree | Neutral | Disagree | Strongly disagree
    5   4   3   2   1

11. I have a savings account in case of an emergency.
    Strongly agree | Agree | Neutral | Disagree | Strongly disagree
    5   4   3   2   1

12. My credit cards are at the maximum limit most of the time.
    Strongly agree | Agree | Neutral | Disagree | Strongly disagree
    5   4   3   2   1

13. I have used Loan Max or Payday loans in an emergency.
    Strongly agree | Agree | Neutral | Disagree | Strongly disagree
    5   4   3   2   1

14. I have a checking account.
    Strongly agree | Agree | Neutral | Disagree | Strongly disagree
    5   4   3   2   1

15. Stewardship presentations have been helpful in managing my finances.
    Strongly agree | Agree | Neutral | Disagree | Strongly disagree
    5   4   3   2   1

16. I use credit cards for most of my purchases.
    Strongly agree | Agree | Neutral | Disagree | Strongly disagree
    5   4   3   2   1

17. I borrow money from friends or relatives.
    Strongly agree | Agree | Neutral | Disagree | Strongly disagree
    5   4   3   2   1

18. My family and friends borrow money from me.
    <u>Strongly agree | Agree | Neutral | Disagree | Strongly disagree</u>
      5   4   3   2   1

19. I overdraw on my checking account.
    <u>Strongly agree | Agree | Neutral | Disagree | Strongly disagree</u>
      5   4   3   2   1

20. Money management is important for my family and me.
    <u>Strongly agree | Agree | Neutral | Disagree | Strongly disagree</u>
      5   4   3   2   1

This Information Will Be Kept Confidential. Please Do Not Place your Name on the Form.

Debt Balances: a. Credit Cards $_____ b. Payday Loans $_____ c. Student Loans $____

APPENDIX H

Wilcoxon Signed Rank Test Results

Rev. Dr. Donna Taylor

Related-Samples Wilcoxon Signed Rank Test

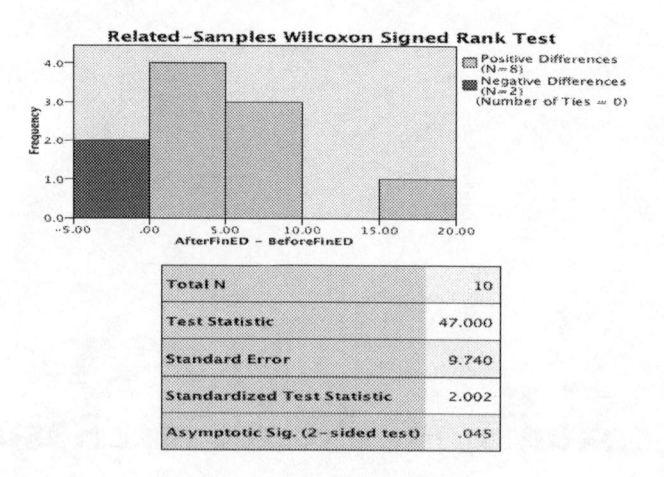

Positive Differences (N=8)
Negative Differences (N=2)
(Number of Ties = 0)

Total N	10
Test Statistic	47.000
Standard Error	9.740
Standardized Test Statistic	2.002
Asymptotic Sig. (2-sided test)	.045

Wilcoxon NonParametric Tests_Financial Literacy Education.sav

Hypothesis Test Summary

	Null Hypothesis	Test	Sig.	Decision
1	The median of differences between BeforeFinED and AfterFinED equals 0.	Related-Samples Wilcoxon Signed Rank Test	.045	Reject the null hypothesis.

Asymptotic significances are displayed. The significance level is .05.

APPENDIX I

Financial Literacy Training

Global Financial Literacy Excellence Center & The Federal Reserve Board Sponsored Financial Literacy Seminar Series (FLSS) – Fall 2013 George Washington University – School of Business

Thursday, September 26, 2013 3:00- 4:00 p.m. – completed 1.5 hours Speaker - Ms. Gerri Walsh, President of the Financial Industry Regulatory Authority (FINRA) Investor Education Foundation Overview of Financial Capability Study. Presentation and panel discussion pertaining to financial capability of Americans based on employment rates, educational status, ability to save, financial fragility, and debt management.

Thursday, October 10, 2013 3:00- 4:00 p.m. – completed 1.5 hours Speaker – Ms. Anna Paulson, Federal Reserve Bank of Chicago High School and Financial Literacy Outcomes. Presentation and discussion to examine a recent study by the Federal Reserve Bank of Chicago that compares High School financial literacy courses with math course outcomes. Math courses provide foster the cognitive acumen of students for financial decision-making.

Thursday, October 24, 2013 3:00- 4:00 p.m. – completed 1.5 hours Speaker - Ms. Julie Agnew, College of William and Mary The increasing extent and complexity of consumer financial decision making has highlighted the need for accessible financial advice. Financial advice has traditionally been the province of wealthier households, but many cannot afford advice under the typical face-to-face, fee-for-service model. The call for inexpensive, mass-market forms of advice is increasing and has public policy implications related to financial advisor certifications and financial education.

Thursday, November 7, 2013
Speaker - Mr. James Choi, Yale University – read white paper There is evidence from field experiments that savings choices are significantly affected by numerical cues. Savings cues present in emails to employees about

their 401(k) savings plan. High savings cues increased 401(k) contribution rates by up to 2.9% of income in a pay period, and low savings cues decreased 401(k) contribution rates by up to 1.4% of income in a pay period. Cues affected 401 (k) contributions rates for up to a year after the email.

Thursday, November 21, 2013

Speaker - Mr. William Skimmyhorn, United States Military Academy – complete 1.5 hours. Assessing Financial Education: Evidence from a Personal Financial Management Course. This research estimates the effects of financial education on a variety of financial outcomes using a large natural experiment within the U.S. Army. The Personal Financial Management Course (PFMC) attendance and enrollment assistance doubles retirement savings, with significant effects throughout the contribution distribution that persist through at least two years. The course has weaker but suggestive effects on credit market outcomes including account balances (credit cards, automobile loans and finance loans) and aggregate monthly credit payments in the first year after soldiers finish their initial job training. Overall, the results suggest that financial education, coupled with assistance and advice, can improve financial outcomes in a number of areas.

Thursday, December 5, 2013

Speaker - Mr. Richard Burkhauser, Cornell University – completed 1.5 hours. Unsustainable growth in program costs and beneficiaries, together with a growing recognition that even people with sever impairments can work, led to fundamental disability policy reforms in the Netherlands, Sweden, and the United Kingdom. These reforms substantially reduced disability recipiency rates in these countries and put their programs back on a sustainable fiscal footing. The United States is now considering fundamental reform of its primary long-term disability cash transfer program, Social Security Disability Insurance (DI).

Resources:
http://business.gwu.edu/flss/
The Steering Committee,
Annamaria Lusardi, George Washington School of Business
John Sabelhaus, Federal Reserve Board
Kristen Burnell, George Washington School of Business
Laura Feiveson, Federal Reserve Board
Joanne Hsu, Federal Reserve Board
Ellen Merry, Federal Reserve Board
Max Schmeiser, Federal Reserve Board
Kamila Sommer, Federal Reserve Board

Tuesday, October 14, 2013- Department of Veterans Affairs (VA) 1.0 hour *Introduction to Social Security in Preparation for Retirement* - Webinar As a component of the Federal Retirement System (FERS) the importance of understanding the requirements to receive benefits for self, spouse, and eligible dependents.

Tuesday, October 22, 2013 -Navy Federal Credit Union –1.0 hour *Women and Money* – Location Vienna, Virginia Financial information for women across life spans and in preparation for purchasing a home, investing for the future, and plans for retirement.

Tuesday, October 22, 2013 - Department of Veterans Affairs (VA) 1.0 hour*Basics of Budgeting* – Webinar Offered simple budgeting principles for individuals with practical application for everyday use.

Wednesday, October 30, 2013 - George Washington University School of Business 1.0 hour Lecture I - Origins and Mission of the Federal Reserve - Webinar viewed 10/30/2013. The Chairman of the

Federal Reserve, Dr. Ben Bernanke explains what central banks do, the origin of central banking in the United States, and the early experience of the Federal Reserve in dealing with a serious financial crisis: the Great Depression.

Thursday, October 31, 2013 – George Washington University School of Business 1.0 hour Lecture II – The Federal Reserve's Response to the Financial Crisis – Webinar viewed 10/31/2013.Chairman Ben Bernanke explains how the financial crisis that emerged in 2007 impacts and influences today's economy and impacts financial literacy knowledge.

Monday, January 27, 2014 – Baptist Ministers Conference of Northern Virginia and Vicinity Meeting 1.0 hour – Mr. Dywane A. Hall, MA, RFC, CRPC, AIF. Financial Literacy Presentation for Ministers to recognize the importance of attaining financial knowledge and understanding strategies to optimize savings for retirement.

Thursday, April 9, 2014 – Financial Boot Camp Part 1 – Department of Veterans Affairs Jeffrey Waters and Maria Geraghty - 1.0 hour Financial boot camp to establish personal financial wellness to review assets, liabilities, and net worth. The facilitator emphasized the importance of monitoring your credit reports annually, managing debt, and savings for emergencies.

Wednesday, April 16, 2014 – Financial Boot Camp Part 2– Department of Veterans Affairs Jeffrey Waters and Maria Geraghty - 1.0 hour Focus on setting financial goals, learning the basics of retirement planning, and asset allocation for retirement accounts/investments. The importance of diversification and reviewing goals periodically to reassess family needs.

Wednesday, April 23, 2014 – Financial Boot Camp Part 3– Department of Veterans Affairs Jeffrey Waters and Maria Geraghty - 1.0 hour Estate planning and assessment of insurance based on the long-term needs of family. The primary breadwinner must plan for family in the event of death of long-term disability. Special emphasis on trust funds, Wills, health proxy, power of attorney, durable and non-durable power of attorney. Selection of a trustworthy executor(s) as an administrator of assets. Select beneficiaries and review periodically as needed.

Wednesday, April 30, 2014 – Financial Boot Camp Part 4– Department of Veterans Affairs Jeffrey Waters and Maria Geraghty – 1 hour. The Psychology of Money requires understanding the importance of developing healthy attitudes about money and its importance in our life. Understand how money makes an individual feel and take a balanced approach to save and spend in moderation. Discuss money issues and concerns with loved ones and to establish ways to function in healthy relationships.

Tuesday, May 6, 2014 – Your Money and Your Career – National Urban League – Webinar Jeanette M. Timmons (financial behaviorist) – 1 hour The four facets of money discussed, which are what we Earn, Spend, Save, and Invest. Each segment is independent yet interdependent. To include the importance of planning ahead, considering oneself as a CEO and the CIO of your career and personal finance; to increase personal confidence; to lead do not push your circumstances. Remember two things. It is never just about money (other factors are involved) and being money smart is a learned skill (the process continues throughout life) www.jacquettetimmons.com/make-money-pleasurable

Wednesday, July 9, 2014 - U.S. Release of the OECD PISA Financial Literacy Assessment of Students – At George Washington University –The Global Financial Literacy Excellence Center – Professor Annamaria Lusardi – 4 hours Programme for International Students Assessment (PISA) was a released and highlighted the importance of providing math, complex problem solving, and teachers equipped to teach financial literacy across several the curriculum. The Secretary of Education Arne Duncan described increasing the rigor within math in the public schools to provide a learning environment conducive to financial literacy. The Chair of the President's Financial Literacy Advisory Council John Rogers emphasized the need for private/public partnerships to bring business leaders into the classroom. Business leaders can also provide financial literacy education through financial products such as stocks and bonds. Richard Cordray of the Consumer Financial Protection Bureau discussed the CFPB role in promoting financial literacy in the public sector as consumers are increasingly required to make complex financial decisions in their daily lives.

APPENDIX J

Financial Empowerment – Marketing Strategy

Rev. Dr. Donna Taylor

Church Clerk Announcements
Church Bulletin Insert
Emails
Text messages
Post cards
Phone calls
Stewardship Emphasis by Deacon Ministry
Face-to-face contacts (personal appeals)
Bible study announcements
Church School Announcements
Pulpit Announcements
Worship Service – Prayer Circle – Announcements

APPENDIX K

Church Bulletin Insert - Early Phase

Rev. Dr. Donna Taylor

First Agape Baptist Community of Faith
Alexandria, VA

Achieve Financial Excellence in 2014!
Achieve Financial Excellence in 2014!
Achieve Financial Excellence in 2014!

Financial Workshop Series

Saturday, January 18th 10:00 a.m. – 12 noon

Saturday, January 25th 10:00 a.m. – 11:30 a.m.

Saturday, February 1st 10:00 a.m. – 11:30 a.m.

Saturday, February 8th 10:00 a.m. – 11:30 a.m.

Saturday, February 15th 10:00 a.m. – 11:30 a.m.

Saturday, February 22nd 10:00 a.m. – 12 noon

Sunday, February 23rd – Award Ceremony

For more information contact Min. Donna Taylor
(703) 347- 2947 (cell)
Email donnawellstaylor@gmail.com

TOPICS: Budgeting| Debt Reduction Principles | R U Credit Card Savvy?

The steps of a righteous man are ordered by the Lord - Psalm 37:23

APPENDIX L

Church Bulletin Insert – Late Phase

Rev. Dr. Donna Taylor

Financial Workshop Series

Saturday, February 22nd 10:00 a.m. – 12 noon

Sunday, February 23rd – Award Ceremony

For more information contact Min. Donna Taylor
(703) 347- 2947 (cell)
Email <donnawellstaylor@gmail.com>

TOPICS:
R U a saver or a spender?
What type of financial legacy will you impart to your children?

The steps of a righteous man are ordered by the Lord - Psalm 37:23

APPENDIX M

Post Card Invitation

It's 2014!
The perfect time to get
Your personal finances
in order!

You have a chance to win $100! Must attend both sessions! Saturday, January 18th and 25th at First Agape Baptist Community of Faith in Alexandria, VA.

*For more information:
Call Minister Donna Taylor 703.347.2947*

APPENDIX N

Email and Text Messages

Rev. Dr. Donna Taylor

Email and Text Messages

Financial Empowerment Workshop - At First Agape - Saturday, Feb. 8th @ 10:00 A.M.

Scheduled for tomorrow on Saturday, February 8th at 10:00 a.m. Hope to see you there!

Peace & Blessings,

Min. Donna Taylor

Financial Workshop at First Agape on Saturday, January 18 & 25 from 10:00 a.m. -2:00 p.m. You have a change to win $ 100 for attending both sessions! Call Minister Donna Taylor to register in advance (703) 347-2947 (cell)

Financial Workshop at First Agape on this Saturday, February 1st from 10:00 a.m. - 1:30 p.m.
Please confirm your availability.
Min. Donna Taylor

APPENDIX O

Workshop #1 God's Blueprint for Personal Finance

Rev. Dr. Donna Taylor

Workshop #1 God's Blueprint for Personal Finance

Slide 1

> **First Agape Baptist Community of Faith Financial Empowerment Series**
> *God's Blueprint for Personal Finance*
>
> Project Director:
> Donna Taylor, Associate Minister
>
> Faculty Advisor:
> Rev. Dr. Daniel L. Brown, Pastor
>
> Facilitators:
> Herbert J. McKoy, Sr., Chair, Deacon Ministry
> David L. Taylor, Vice Chair, Deacon Ministry

Slide 2

> **Learning Objectives**
> At the completion of the workshop, learners will be able to:
>
> - Discuss key scriptures illustrating God's wealth
> - Explain God's order for managing financial blessings
> - Apply biblical principles in our financial decisions

Slide 3

> **Small Group Activity**
>
> MONEYTREE

Slide 4

God's Word On Finance

- Psalms 112:3 *Wealth and riches are in his house, and his righteousness endures forever.*
- Philippians 4:19 *And my God will supply every need of yours according to his riches in glory in Christ Jesus.*
- Matthew 6:33 *But seek first the kingdom of God and his righteousness, and all these things will be added to you.*

Slide 5

God's Word On Finance

- Matthew 6:21 *For where your treasure is, there your heart will be also.*
- Proverbs 3:9 *Honor the Lord with your wealth and with the first fruits of all your produce.*
- Galatians 6:10 *Therefore, as we have opportunity, let us do good to all people, especially to those who belong to the family of believers.*

Slide 6

God's Order For Finance

1 Corinthians 14:40 But everything should be done in a fitting and orderly way

- Tither: Honor God out of love and obedience (Luke 10:27 & Malachi 3:10)
- Steward: Honor God as a trustworthy manager of resources (1 Corinthians 4:2 & Colossians 3:23).

Rev. Dr. Donna Taylor

Slide 7

God & Financial Decisions
- Receive God's word as truth, knowing that He is pleased with your obedience. (2 Timothy 2:15)
- Follow God's plan in all decisions with discipline. (Tutus 2:7)
- Your decisions should honor and glorify God (Colossians 3:17)

Slide 8

God & Financial Decisions
- God requires an accounting of the finances He has entrusted to us. (Luke 16:10-11)
- A written budget will help master finances, not become a slave to finances (Matthew 6:24)
- Apply God's principles to reflect His grace and blessing (2 Corinthians 9:7-8)

Slide 9

A LOOK at the BUDGET

Slide 10

God's Blueprint for Personal Finance

➤ God owns everything! He blesses us with financial resources to care for our families and to spread His gospel.

➤ God expects us to follow his plan for our finances, and He shares with us the responsibilities of His steward.

➤ God desires that we use His word as the guide for our personal finance.

APPENDIX P

Workshop #2 Godly Tools for Debt Prevention

Rev. Dr. Donna Taylor

Workshop #2 God's Tools for Debt Prevention

Slide 1

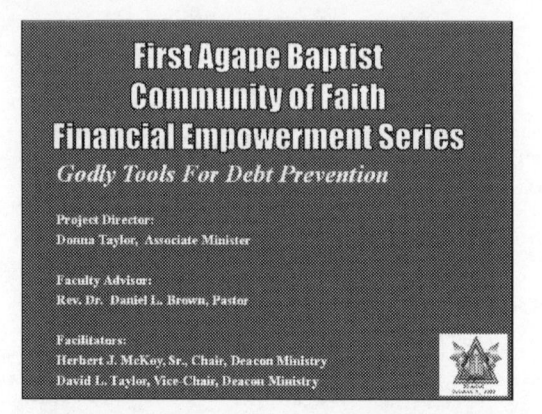

> **First Agape Baptist Community of Faith Financial Empowerment Series**
> *Godly Tools For Debt Prevention*
>
> Project Director:
> Donna Taylor, Associate Minister
>
> Faculty Advisor:
> Rev. Dr. Daniel L. Brown, Pastor
>
> Facilitators:
> Herbert J. McKoy, Sr., Chair, Deacon Ministry
> David L. Taylor, Vice-Chair, Deacon Ministry

Slide 2

> **Learning Objectives**
> At the completion of the workshop, learners will be able to:
> • Discuss key scriptures illustrating the pitfalls of debt
> • Create a budget to prevent debt using God's order for finance
> • Create a plan to eliminate debt and restore a positive credit rating

Slide 3

> **Small Group Activity**

Financial Empowerment in the African American Church

Slide 4

God's Word On Debt

- Proverbs 3:27: *Do not withhold good from those to whom it is due, when it is in your power to act.*
- Luke 12:15: *"Watch out! Be on your guard against all kinds of greed; life does not consist in an abundance of possessions."*
- Romans 13:8: *Let no debt remain outstanding, except the continuing debt to love one another, for whoever loves others has fulfilled the law*

Slide 5

Small Group Activity

Slide 6

God's Order For Finance

- Tithe: Malachi 3:10: *Bring the whole tithe into the storehouse, that there may be food in my house. Test me in this," says the LORD Almighty, "and see if I will not throw open the floodgates of heaven and pour out so much blessing that there will not be room enough to store it.*
- Taxes, Family Expenses, Savings, Debt Reduction, Fellowship

Slide 8

God's Financial Freedom

> *Philippians 4:19: And my God will meet all your needs according to the riches of his glory in Christ Jesus.*
> *Proverbs 8:20-21: I walk in the way of righteousness, along the paths of justice, bestowing a rich inheritance on those who love me and making their treasuries full.*
> *Hebrews 13:5: Keep your lives free from the love of money and be content with what you have, because God has said, "Never will I leave you; nor ever will I forsake you."*

Slide 9

Small Group Activity

ROAD TO GOOD CREDIT

What's Your SCORE?
Average US Credit Score is 678
Excellent: 750 and up
Good: 720 - 749
Fair: 680 - 719 ---- 678
Uncertain: 620 - 659
Poor: 619 or lower

Slide 10

Godly Tools For Debt Prevention

> *God instructs us to minimize debt, so only the debt of love remains for one another.*
> *God expects us to follow His plan for our finances, setting a budget with His tithe as the first responsibility.*
> *God desires abundance for us, and His plan for financial freedom will always result in more Blessings!*

APPENDIX Q

Workshop #3 Godly Tools for Debt Management

Rev. Dr. Donna Taylor

Slide 1

> **First Agape Baptist Community of Faith Financial Empowerment Series**
> *Godly Tools For Debt Prevention*
>
> Project Director:
> Donna Taylor, Associate Minister
>
> Faculty Advisor:
> Rev. Dr. Daniel L. Brown, Pastor
>
> Facilitators:
> Herbert J. McKoy, Sr., Chair, Deacon Ministry
> David L. Taylor, Vice-Chair, Deacon Ministry

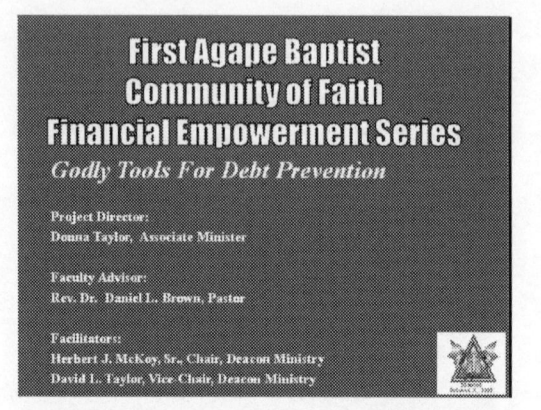

Slide 2

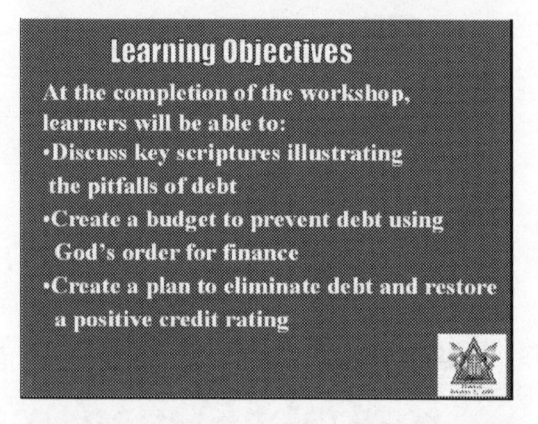

> **Learning Objectives**
> At the completion of the workshop, learners will be able to:
> • Discuss key scriptures illustrating the pitfalls of debt
> • Create a budget to prevent debt using God's order for finance
> • Create a plan to eliminate debt and restore a positive credit rating

Slide 3

> **Small Group Activity**
>
> Need Cash?
> We're Here to Help.
> 1 It's Easy
> 2 It's Safe
> 3 Get up to **$1500**

Slide 4

Financial Literacy Towards Debt Management
- Knowledge and understanding of matters involving financial planning, extension of credit, debt reduction and methods of saving and investment
- Personal decisions and models on handling financial matters
- Skills and discipline to implement financial strategies.

Slide 5

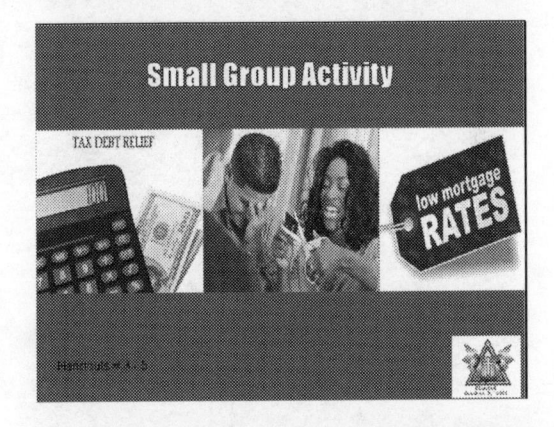

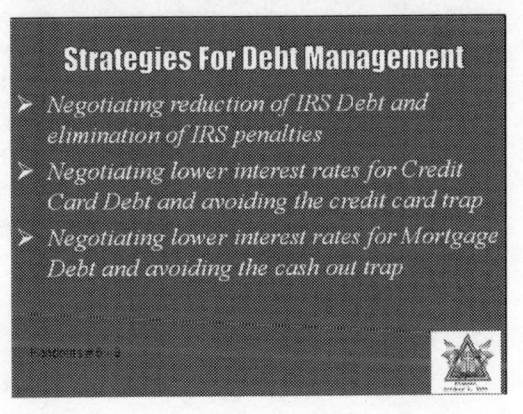

Small Group Activity

Slide 6

Strategies For Debt Management
- Negotiating reduction of IRS Debt and elimination of IRS penalties
- Negotiating lower interest rates for Credit Card Debt and avoiding the credit card trap
- Negotiating lower interest rates for Mortgage Debt and avoiding the cash out trap

Rev. Dr. Donna Taylor

Slide 7

God's Debt Management Plan
- Ecclesiastes 5:5: It is better not to make a vow than to make one and not fulfill it.
- Proverbs 28:20: A faithful person will be richly blessed, but one eager to get rich will not go unpunished.
- Luke 12:15b: "Watch out and guard yourselves from every kind of greed; because your true life is not made up of the things you own, no matter how rich you may be."

Slide 8

God's Debt Management Plan
- Philippians 4:19: And my God will meet all your needs according to the riches of his glory in Christ Jesus.
- Hebrews 13:5: Keep your lives free from the love of money and be content with what you have, because God has said, "Never will I leave you; nor ever will I forsake you."

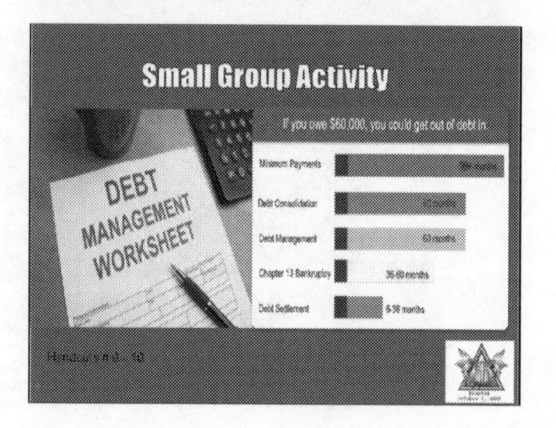

Slide 9

Small Group Activity

Slide 10

Godly Tools For Debt Management

➤ God instructs us to minimize debt, so only the debt of love remains for one another.

➤ God expects us to follow His plan for our finances, which creates discipline to avoid "debt traps".

➤ God is faithful to supply all of our needs, and His order for finances will always result in more Blessings!

APPENDIX R

Workshop #4 A Godly Plan: Saving for Emergencies

Rev. Dr. Donna Taylor

Workshop#4 Godly Plan for Saving for Emergencies

Slide 1

First Agape Baptist Community of Faith Financial Empowerment Series
A Godly Plan: Saving For Emergencies

Project Director:
Donna Taylor, Associate Minister

Faculty Advisor:
Rev. Dr. Daniel L. Brown, Pastor

Facilitators:
Herbert J. McKoy, Sr., Chair, Deacon Ministry
David L. Taylor, Vice Chair, Deacon Ministry

Slide 2

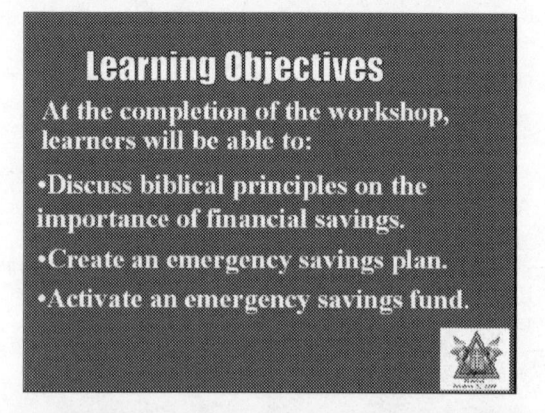

Learning Objectives

At the completion of the workshop, learners will be able to:

- Discuss biblical principles on the importance of financial savings.
- Create an emergency savings plan.
- Activate an emergency savings fund.

Slide 3

Small Group Activity

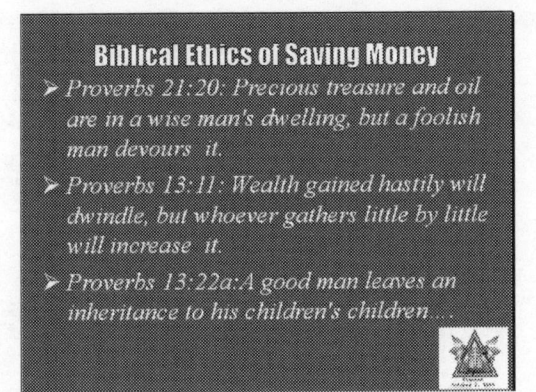

Financial Empowerment in the African American Church

Slide 4

Biblical Ethics of Saving Money
- *Proverbs 21:20: Precious treasure and oil are in a wise man's dwelling, but a foolish man devours it.*
- *Proverbs 13:11: Wealth gained hastily will dwindle, but whoever gathers little by little will increase it.*
- *Proverbs 13:22a: A good man leaves an inheritance to his children's children....*

Slide 5

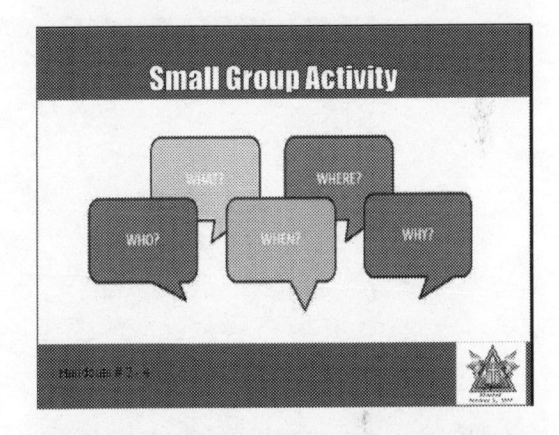

Small Group Activity

WHAT? WHERE? WHO? WHEN? WHY?

Slide 6

Small Group Activity

MONEY AV / SAVINGS ST

Rev. Dr. Donna Taylor

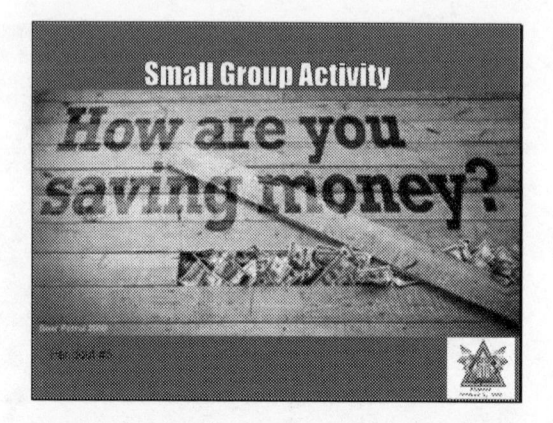

Slide 7

Small Group Activity
How are you saving money?

Slide 8

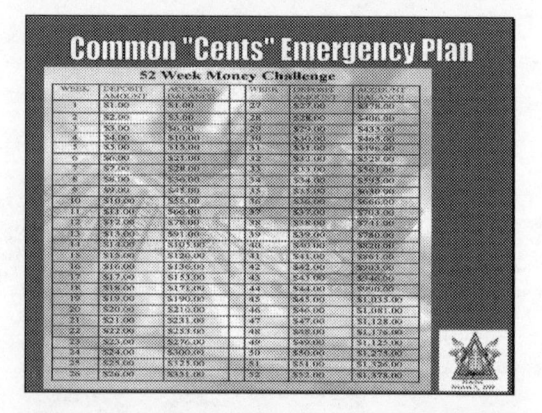

Common "Cents" Emergency Plan
52 Week Money Challenge

Slide 9

Godly Money "Savers"

➤ *Philippians 4:19: And my God will meet all your needs according to the riches of his glory in Christ Jesus.*

➤ *Hebrews 13:5: Keep your lives free from the love of money and be content with what you have, because God has said, "Never will I leave you; nor ever will I forsake you."*

Slide 10

Godly Reminders For Saving

- God owns everything, and we are stewards of what He has entrusted to us.
- We must honor God by saving in a manner consistent with the principles of finance presented in scripture.
- God is faithful to supply all of our needs, and His order for finances will help us save in good and challenging times.

APPENDIX S

Workshop #5 Estate Planning: Family Dialogue & Legacy

Rev. Dr. Donna Taylor

Workshop #5 Estate Planning: Family Dialogue & Legacy

Slide 1

> **First Agape Baptist Community of Faith Financial Empowerment Series**
> *Estate Planning: Family Dialogue & Legacy*
>
> Project Director:
> Donna Taylor, Associate Minister
>
> Faculty Advisor:
> Rev. Dr. Daniel L. Brown, Pastor
>
> Facilitators:
> Herbert J. McKoy, Sr., Chair, Deacon Ministry
> David L. Taylor, Vice-Chair, Deacon Ministry

Slide 2

> **Learning Objectives**
> At the completion of the workshop, learners will be able to:
> • Discuss biblical principles on the importance of estate planning.
> • Discuss the essential components of an estate plan.
> • Implement family dialogue and legacy activities for estate plan.

Slide 3

> **Small Group Activity**
> "We make a living by what we get, but we make a life by what we give."
> — Winston Churchill
>
> Handout #1

Financial Empowerment in the African American Church

Slide 4

Biblical Principles of Estate Planning

➢ *Proverbs 13:22a:* "*A good man leaves an inheritance to his children's children...*"

➢ *Ephesians 1:11:* "*All things are done according to God's plan and decision; and God chose us to be his own people in union with Christ because of his own purpose, based on what he had decided from the very beginning.*"

Slide 5

Biblical Principles of Estate Planning

➢ *Proverb 14:15:* "*The naive believes everything, but the sensible man considers his steps*"

➢ *Proverbs 22:6:* "*Train up a child in the way he should go, even when he is old he will not depart from it*"

Slide 6

Small Group Activity

ESTATE PLANNING

Rev. Dr. Donna Taylor

Slide 7

Three Essential Steps For Estate Planning
- Set Priority Time To Document
- Set Priority Time To Discuss
- Set Priority Time To Update

Slide 8

Small Group Activity

Slide 9

Family Dialogue & Legacy Activities
- Use family meals, reunions and special meeting requests to discuss general and specific information for your estate.
- Initiate mentoring opportunities across three generations to sustain family blessings.
- Initiate family legacy gifts.

Slide 10

Family Dialogue & Legacy Activities
- *Use family meals, reunions and special meeting requests to discuss general and specific information for your estate.*
- *Initiate mentoring opportunities across three generations to sustain family blessings.*
- *Initiate family legacy gifts.*

APPENDIX T

Workshop#6 Applying Stewardship and Debt Management Principles

Rev. Dr. Donna Taylor

Slide 1

First Agape Baptist Community of Faith Financial Empowerment Series
Applying Stewardship & Debt Management Principles

Project Director:
Donna Taylor, Associate Minister

Faculty Advisor:
Rev. Dr. Daniel L. Brown, Pastor

Facilitators:
Herbert J. McKoy, Sr., Chair, Deacon Ministry
David L. Taylor, Vice Chair, Deacon Ministry

Slide 2

Learning Objectives
At the completion of the workshop, learners will be able to:
- Summarize biblical principles on debt management and financial stewardship.
- Apply Christian decision making skills to reduce consumer debt.
- Create short and long term financial goals.

Slide 3

Workshop 1
God's Blueprint For Personal Finance

Matthew 6:33
But seek first the kingdom of God and his righteousness, and all these things will be added to you.

Financial Empowerment in the African American Church

Slide 4

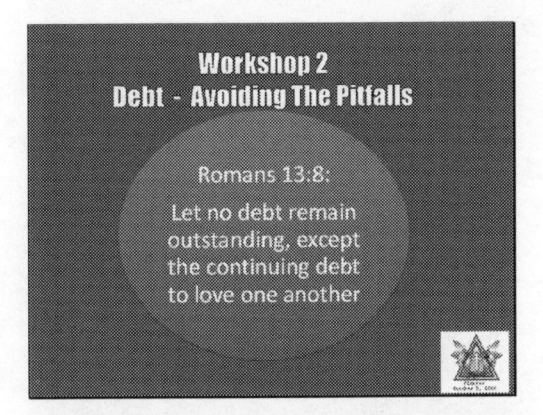

> **Workshop 2**
> **Debt - Avoiding The Pitfalls**
>
> Romans 13:8:
> Let no debt remain outstanding, except the continuing debt to love one another

Slide 5

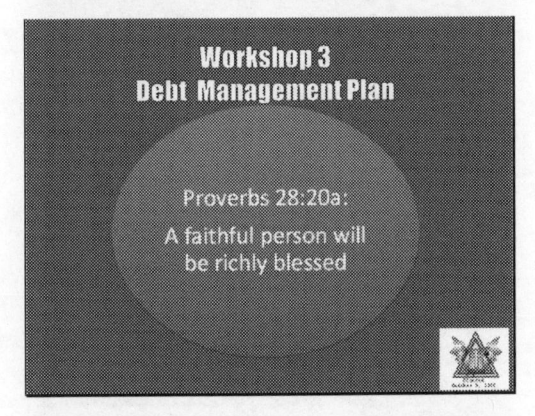

> **Workshop 3**
> **Debt Management Plan**
>
> Proverbs 28:20a:
> A faithful person will be richly blessed

Slide 6

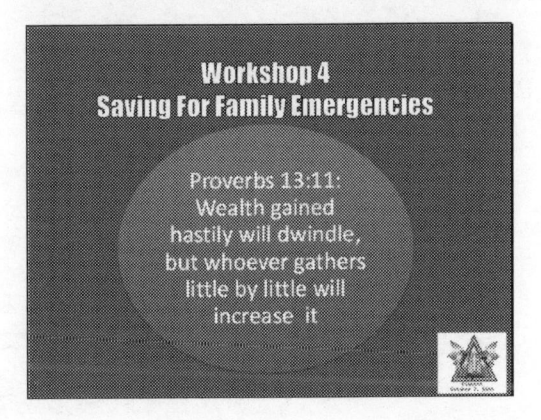

> **Workshop 4**
> **Saving For Family Emergencies**
>
> Proverbs 13:11:
> Wealth gained hastily will dwindle, but whoever gathers little by little will increase it

Slide 7

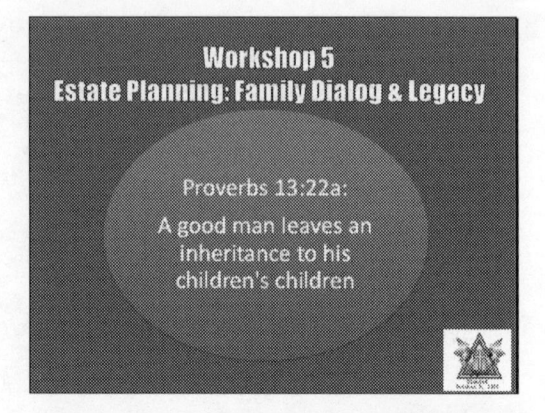

**Workshop 5
Estate Planning: Family Dialog & Legacy**

Proverbs 13:22a:
A good man leaves an inheritance to his children's children

Slide 8

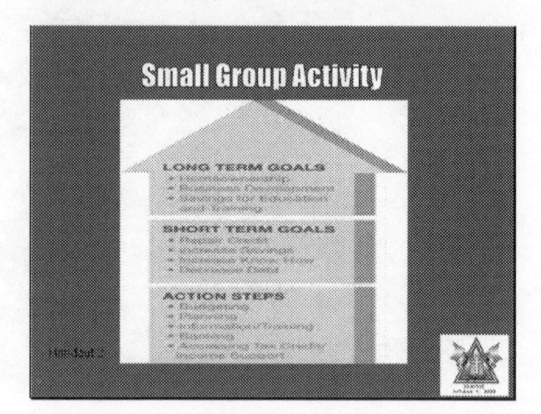

Small Group Activities

Slide 9

Small Group Activity

LONG TERM GOALS
- Homeownership
- Business Development
- Savings for Education and Training

SHORT TERM GOALS
- Repair Credit
- Increase Savings
- Increase Know How
- Decrease Debt

ACTION STEPS
- Budgeting
- Planning
- Information/Training
- Banking
- Accessing Tax Credits/Income Support

Slide 10

Christian Financial Empowerment

➢ *We are stewards of the Blessings that God has entrusted to us.*
➢ *We honor God by establishing financial plans according to His scriptures.*
➢ *We reap God's Blessings and avoid debt by establishing a budget and savings plan to perpetuate His Blessings to future generations.*

APPENDIX U

Participants' Comments at the Conclusion of the Financial Empowerment Workshop

Participants' Comments At the Conclusion of the Financial Empowerment Workshop

The participant's comments included a plan to save $25/month of my income. To pay off large debt and add more money to a small debt and when that debt is paid off then the amount that you were paying on that debt can be added to the larger remaining debt to allow a swifter payoff timeframe.

To pay off credit cards by communicating with the creditors and paying off the smaller debts first then take that same amount and apply it to the remaining debts.

To reduce debt I will start by looking at my credit report.

To pay off the most manageable debt, and when that is paid off, add to the next bill and to increase the lumps sums applied to each subsequent payment.
Call creditors to see if they will lower my interest rates.

Save by using a chart and budget my income by using coupons, find sales, keep all receipts, and keep track of my spending habits.

Plan to make a will to leave my assets to family members and speak with a lawyer to discuss my will.

Ask God to help me to cease from getting into debt by seeking things I want instead of things I need.

Learn to save weekly or monthly in small increments and discuss estate planning with family members and prepare a will.

Seek ye first the kingdom of heaven, and these things will be added unto you. Try to leave an inheritance for our children and the church.

Set goals to save money and put my trust in the Lord.

Save a set amount every per pay period.

Avoid using title loans.

BIBLIOGRAPHY

American Association of African American Financial Advisors. *AAAFAinc. org* www.aaafainc.com accessed on May 7, 2013.

Ammerman, N.T., Carroll, J.W., Dudley, C. S., Eiesland, N. L. et al., 1998. *Studying Congregations – A New Handbook,* Abington Press Nashville.

Babbie, E. 2008. *The Basics of Social Research,* Chapman University, Thomson and Wadsworth, 4th Edition.

Bell, Elizabeth and Robert I. Lerman. 2005. *Can Financial Literacy Enhance Asset Building? Urban Institute,* No. 6.

. 2006.*Financial Literacy Strategies: Where Do We Go From Here?* Opportunity and Ownership Project, Report No.1, *The Urban Institute.*

Bennett Jr., Leone. 1982. *Before the Mayflower – A History of Black America,* Penguin Books, 6th Edition.

Blake Jr., Joseph M. and Jelena Vucetic. 2013. *The Influence of Financial Literacy on Faith-Based Epistemology: A Case Study of Arizona Church Members,* International Journal of Social Science Research.

Boston, Kelvin. 1996. *Smart Money Moves for African Americans,* C.P. Putnam's Sons.

Brayboy, Larry. 2012. *The Black Church in America – Preparing for a New Century,* Popular Truth Publishing.

Bryant, John H. 2009. *Love Leadership: The New Way to Lead In a Fear-Based World.*

Jossey-Bassey, A Wiley Imprint.

Brown, Daniel L. 2013, *Church Planting,* Red Lead Press.

Building Economic Security in America's Cities: *New Municipal Strategies for Asset Building and Financial Empowerment.* 2011. CFED (Corporation For Enterprise Development), Executive Summary.

Bullock, Lorinda. 2006. *The High Cost of Being Poor, Carolina Peacemaker,* Black PressUSA Network http://www.carolinapeacemaker.com assessed on September 17, 2012.

Burkett, Larry.1975. *How To Manage Your Money – An In-depth Bible Study on Personal Finances, The Christian Financial Concept Series,* Moody Press

Capra, T. 2009. *Poverty and It's Impact on Education: Today and Tomorrow, Thought and Action.* NEA Education Journal.

Cole, S., Paulson, A. Shastry, G.K. 2014. *High School Curriculum and Financial Outcomes: The Impact of Mandated Personal Financial Mathematical Courses.* HarvardBusiness School.

Coombs, G. K., Anderson, L., Dowie, J. M. 2012, *Alexandria - Images of America, Arcadia Publishing, 2012.*

Creswell, J. W. 2009. *Research Design – Qualitative, Quantitative, and Mixed Methods Approaches,* University of Nebraska- Lincoln, Sage Publications, 3rd Edition.

Cronk, B. C. 2010. *How to Use PASW Statistics – A Step-by-Step Guide to Analysis and Interpretation*. Sixth Edition. Pyrczak Publishing.

Doctor of Ministry Manual 2011- 2012. *Virginia University of Lynchburg, School of Religion*.

Duong, J., Condon, A., Taylor, K., Torres, M., Daniels, L. et al., 2014, *Banking In Color: New Findings on Financial Access for Low and Moderate Income Communities,* The National Coalition for Asian Pacific American Community

Development (National CAPACD), National Urban League, and La Raza.

Etzel, B.J. 2003. *Webster's New World Finance and Investment Dictionary*, Wiley Publishers.

Fink, A. 2003. *How to Ask Survey Questions,* Sage Publications, 2nd Edition.

Forté, Karin S., Taylor, Edward W., Tisdell, Elizabeth J., Imel, Susan, and Ross-Gordon,

Jovita M. 2014. *New Directions for Adult and Continuing Education – Financial Literacy and Adult Education,* Number 141, Jossey-Bass Publishers.

Friedman, Bob., Ying Shi, Sarah Rosen Wartell. 2012. Savings: The Poor Can Save, Too, *Democracy: A Journal of Ideas,* Issue #26. http://www.democracyjournal.org/26/savings-the-poor-can-save-too.php accessed on September 17, 2012.

Friedman, Pamela. 2005. *Providing and Funding Financial Literacy Programs for Low-Income Adults and Youth,* The Finance Project.

Gale, William G. and Ruth Levine. 2010. *Financial Literacy: What Works? How Could It Be More Effective?* Urban-Brookings Tax policy Center, Brookings Institute. http://www.brookings.edu/research/

papers/2012/10/financial-literacy-gale-levine accessed November 20, 2012.

Gallmeyer, Alice and Wade T. Roberts. 2009. *Payday lenders and economically distressed communities: A Spatial Analysis of Financial Predation*, The Social Science Journal.

George Washington School of Business, Financial Literacy Seminar Series (FLSS) http://business.gwu.edu/faculty/annamaria_lusardi.cfm accessed on June 15, 2014.

Green, Samuel B. and Salkind, Neil, J. 2011. *Using SPSS for Windows and Macintosh: Analyzing and Understanding Data,* Prentice Hall, Sixth Edition.

Greene, Kenneth R. 2012. *Racism: Its Impact on the African American Family,* Leaven Publishers, Vol. 6. Issue 2, Article 9.

Greenwood, D. J. and Levin, M. 1998. *Introduction to Action Research, Social Research for Social Change,* Sage Publications.

Harriman's Financial Dictionary, Edited by Simon Briscoe and Jane Fuller, Harriman House, 2013.

Harris, A. L. 2010. *The Economic and Educational State of Black Americans in the 21st Century: Should We Be Optimistic or Concerned?* The Review of the Black Policitcal Economy.

Hollander, M., Wolfe, D.A., and Chicken, E. 2014. *Nonparametric Statistical Methods,* John Wiley & Sons, Inc.

Jakes, T.D. 2000. *The Great Investment – Faith, Family, and Finance.* C. P. Putnam's Sons.

Jecewiz. Dana 2013. *Building Community Through Communicaiton: A Look A UHM's Financial Literacy Program,* New York Univeristy. http://

danajecewiz.weebly.com/uploads/1/8/0/0/18001767/d.jecewiz-financial_literacy.pdf Accessed on August 8, 2014.

Joyner, Ronnie D. 1993. *Breaking Free From Financial Bondage – A Biblical Plan to Take Control of Your Finances,* Ronnie D. Joyner, Ministries, Inc.

Jump$tart Coalition for Personal Literacy. 2004. *Personal Financial Survey of High School Seniors,* Executive Summary: Jump$tart Coalition for Personal Literacy, www.jump$tart.org assessed on November 29, 2012.

Kane, Mary. 2012. *For Financial Literacy, A Surprising Political War,* Alica Patterson Foundation, http://aliciapatterson.org/stories/financial-literacy-surprising-political-war, accessed on December 12, 2012.

Kunkler, Duke. 2013. *Financial Literacy – Timeless Concepts to Turn Financial Chaos into Clarity,* Kunkler.

Lerman, Robert I. and Bell, Elizabeth. 2005. *Can Financial Literacy Enhance Asset Building?* Opportunity and Ownership. The Urban Institute. No. 6.

. 2006. *Financial Literacy Strategies: Where Do We Go From Here?* Opportunity and Ownership Project, Report No. 1, The Urban Institute.

Lincoln, Karen D. 2007. *Financial Strain; Negative Interactions; Personal Mastery, Pathways to Mental Health in Older African Americans,* Journal of Black Psychology, 33, 439.

Lowe, Phillip. 2008. *The Challenge of the New Economy & the Threat of Economic Collapse,* Black Wallstreet www.blackwallstreet.org accessed on December 7, 2012.

Lowrey, C. and Taylor, S. 2011. *The African American Financial Experience, The* Prudential Research Study., Prudential Financial, Inc.

Lusardi, A. 2004. *Saving and the Effectiveness of Financial Education, In Pension Design And Structure: New Lessons from Behavioral Finance.* Edited by Oliva Mitchell and Stephen Utkus. New York: Oxford University Press.

. 2005. *Financial Education and the Saving Behavior of African-American and Hispanic Households,* Department of Economics Dartmouth. College Hanover, New Hampshire.

. 2009. *National Financial Capability Study in the United States,* Initial Report, National Survey, Applied Research and Consulting, LLC.

. 2009. *The Importance of Financial Literacy,* National Bureau of Economic Research, *NBER Reporter: Research Summary* 2009 Number 2, www.nber.org/reporter/2009number2/lusardi.htm assessed online on September 12, 2012.

Lusardi, A. and C. D. B. Scheresburg. 2013. *Financial Literacy and the High Cost of Borrowing in the United States,* National Bureau of Economic Research, FINRA Investor Education Foundation.

Lusardi, A. and Mitchell, O. 2014. *The Economic Importance of Financial Literacy: Theory and Evidence,* Journal of Economic Literature.

Mandell, L. 2004. *State of Financial Literacy of Young African-American Adults in America,* Special Report Commissioned by Operation HOPE, Inc. State University of New York at Buffalo and the Jump$tart Coalition for Personal Financial Literacy Based Upon a Survey Sponsored by Merrill-Lynch.

Martz, Catharyn, *Dictionary of Investment Terms,* Texere Thomson/South-Western Corporation, 2006.

McKernan, Signe-Mary and Caroline Racliffe. 2008. *Enabling Families to Weather Emergencies and Develop: The Role of Assests,* The Urban Institue, New Safety Net Paper 7.

McKernan, Signe-Mary, Caroline Racliffe, Trina Williams Shanks. 2012. *Can the Poor Accumulate Assets?* Urban Institute, No. 23.

Myers, W. R. 1997. *Research in Ministry: A Primer for the Doctor of Ministry Program*, Exploration Press.

National Credit Union Administration – www.ncua.gov

National Foundation of Credit Counseling. 2011. *Consumer Financial Literacy Survey Final Report*. Harris Interactive Inc., Public Relations Research. 7.

Oliver, M. L. and Thomas M. Shapiro. 1997. *Black Wealth and White Wealth: A New Perspective on Racial Inequality*, Routledge New York and London.

Osili, Una et al., 2013. *The 2013 Congregational Economic Impact Study*, Indiana University School of Philanthropy and Lake Institute On Faith and Giving.

Personal Financial Management Course: *Your Start to a Fresh Financial Future*. www.DebtorEdu.com assessed on September 17, 2012.

Ramsey, D. 2013. *The Total Money Makeover: Classic Edition: A Proven Plan for Financial Fitness*, Thomas Nelson Publishers.

Ratcliff, C. 2008. *Enabling Families to Weather Emergencies and Develop the Role of Assets*, Urban Institute, New Safety Net Paper 7.

Reavis, R. et al. 2011-2012. *Virginia University of Lynchburg: Doctor of Ministry Program*, Virginia University of Lynchburg.

Reavis, R. 2012. *Apostles of Self-Help and Independence: Chronicles of History*, Publishers Solutions.

Saunders, Lauren K., Leah A. Plunkett, Caroline Carter. 2010. *Stopping the Payday Loan*

Trap: Alternatives That Work, Ones That Don't, National Consumer Law Center.

Schwartz, Michael A. 2010. *Martin Luther King's Atlanta Church Adds Financial Literacy Training*, USA TODAY online. http://usatoday30.usatoday.com/news/religion/2010-04-09kingchurch8_ST_N.htm accessed on September 20, 2012.

Scott, Ellsworth. 1982. *Death in a Promised Land,* Louisiana State University Press, 1982.

Seidman, E. Hababou, M. and Kramer, J. 2005. *Getting to Know the Unbanked Consumers: A Financial Services Analysis,* The Center for Financial Services Innovation - An Initiative of ShoreBank Advisory Services.

Singletary, M. 2006. *Your Money and Your Man - How You and Prince Charming Can Spend Well and Live Rich,* Random House.

Skiba, P.M. and Tobacman, J. 2007. *Do Payday Loans Cause Bankruptcy?* Horowitz Foundation and the Harvard Economics Department.

Soaries Jr., DeForest B. 2010. *Black Churches and the Prosperity Gospel: Depending on miracles as a financial strategy is a dangerous way to live.* Wall Street Journal online http://online.wsj.com/article/SB10001424052748704116004575522202425314706.html accessed on November 20, 2012.

.2011. *dfree Breaking Free from Financial Slavery,* Zondervan Publishers

State of the African American Consumer. 2011. *National Newspapers Association. Nielsen Company* and National Newspaper Publishing Association/ Black Press USA.

Stephens, Brooke. 1997. *Talking Dollars and Making Sense – A Wealth Building Guide for African-Americans,* McGraw-Hill Publishers.

Taylor, Gardner C. 2014. *Concord Baptist Church of Christ,* Bedford Stuyvesant, Brooklyn, New York http://www.concordcares.org/about-us/history

Taylor, P., Kochar, R., Fry, R., Velasco, G., and Motel, S. 2011. *Wealth Gaps Rise to Record Highs Between Whites, Blacks and Hispanics*, Pew Research Center, Social & Demographic Trends. *The National Black Church Initiative Launches a Historic Savings Program for the Black Community*. Washington, D.C. www.naltblackchurch.com *The New Oxford American Dictionary*, Oxford University Press, Second Edition, 2005.

Turabian, K. L. 2007. *A Manual for Writers of Research Papers, Theses, and Dissertations*, University of Chicago Press Editorial Staff, 7th Edition.

Urahn, Susan K. 2012. *Pew Payday Lending in America: Who Borrows, Where They Borrow and Why, the Pew Charitable Trusts*, Pew Research..

U. S. President. 2010. Executive Order no. 13530. *President's Advisory Council on Financial Capability*, White House, Office of the Press Secretary. Federal Register Vol. 75, No. 22, http://www.whitehouse.gov/the-press-office/exceutive-order-presidents-advisory-council-financial-capability accessed on November 20, 2012.

Vitt et al. 2001. *Personal Finance and the Rush to Competence: Financial Literacy Education in the U.S.*, Fannie Mae Foundation, and Institute for Socio-Financial Studies.

Vitt, Lois. 2009. *Values-Centered Financial Education Understanding Cultural Influences On Learners' Financial Behaviors*, The Institute for Socio-Financial Studies (ISFS) And The National Endowment for Financial Education (NEFE).

Walsh, G. 2013. *National Financial Capability Study Findings*, Financial Industry Regulatory Authority (FINRA), Investor Education Foundation.

White, Randy. 2013. *Starving Payday Lenders: Targeted Faith-Centered Financial Literacy Training in a Context of Concentrated Poverty,* Transform Central Valley, California http://transformcentralvalley.org accessed on August 1, 2013.

Xiao, Jing, J. et al. 2001. *Application of the Transtheoretical Model of Change to Financial Behavior,* Consumer Interest, Annual Volume.

Printed in the United States
By Bookmasters